Advance Praise

"*ADHD Refocused* makes good on the promise in its title. Dr. Sitt brings to bear not only his professional experience but also his personal experience in this lucid, practical, and warmhearted book. Sitt has lived through the ADHD triumphs and travails. With this book he hands the reader a wonderfully written and clearly reasoned account of what he's learned along the way. I highly recommend this book."

—EDWARD HALLOWELL, MD, AUTHOR OF
DRIVEN TO DISTRACTION AND *ADHD 2.0*

"*If you have ADHD or someone you care about has it, this is a must-read! David Sitt beautifully weaves compelling stories, rigorous science, and practical advice to present a picture of ADHD that is both realistic and optimistic.*"

—TAL BEN-SHAHAR, PhD, BESTSELLING AUTHOR
OF *HAPPIER, NO MATTER WHAT*, CHIEF LEARNING
OFFICER AT HAPPINESS STUDIES ACADEMY

"Dr. Sitt gets it just right in this book. He does a great job explaining life with ADHD in relatable and understandable ways but, maybe more importantly, shares the strategies that will help you live that better life. He brings a mix of personal experience, clinical skills, and academic foundation to create a readable and useful book. Check it out."

—ARI TUCKMAN, PsyD, ADHD EXPERT,
AUTHOR, AND INTERNATIONAL SPEAKER

ADHD Refocused

ADHD Refocused

Bringing Clarity to the Chaos

David Sitt, PsyD

LIONCREST
PUBLISHING

ADHD REFOCUSED
Bringing Clarity to the Chaos

FIRST EDITION

ISBN   978-1-5445-0730-9 *Hardcover*
   978-1-5445-0634-0 *Paperback*
   978-1-5445-0635-7 *Ebook*
   978-1-5445-4307-9 *Audiobook*

To my parents, Eddie[A"H] and Frieda Sitt, for their unwavering and unconditional support.

To my children, Ezra, Jonah, Natan, and Frieda—I hope this book will serve as a small inspiration to overcome whatever challenges cross your path on the way to your dreams.

To my wife, Ayla—thank you for helping me refocus on what matters most each and every day.

Contents

Author's Note

What follows includes stories of my experience as both a practitioner and a person with ADHD. Wherever those stories include client relationships or anyone other than myself, I have changed the names and details to protect confidentiality. In some cases, I created an amalgamation rather than relying on specific individual stories. These are meant to be realistic anecdotes, and the spirit of each remains true enough that I hope you see yourself in them. Any overlap with real-life situations beyond that relatability is otherwise coincidental.

Introduction

In typical ADHD fashion, I hacked this book into existence.

After twenty years of knowing I should write a book, and nearly half of that spent procrastinating and dipping my pinkie toe into the treacherous water of writing, I finally seized an impulse to plan once again for the end zone, this time through a brilliant company called Scribe. There, I enlisted the help of a full team of talented people to help me bring my ideas to these pages.

The first phase matched me with a scribe who reviewed all of my previous ADHD-related writings, recordings, and scribbles, and who conducted interviews with me regarding my content. Over the course of several months, he sifted, organized, and helped me produce my first draft. In phase two, I worked with a second scribe on edits, rewrites, and refinements in a very hands-on, collaborative process. In the final stages, we polished the manuscript, got marketing and media materials together, and went to print.

For a moment, I considered keeping this process as backdrop or perhaps a small footnote, but I now realize how proud I am of this path. It effectively models the way I have come to organize my personal challenges of living with ADHD. Writing is still agony, but working with a team got me to the finish line. By using tools and techniques like the Scribe Method, we can increase our probabilities of success, appreciate 80 as the new 100, and balance our *nows* vs *not nows* to accomplish more and with less resistance than we could by just powering through.

These days, attention deficit hyperactivity disorder seems so commonplace that we use its acronym, ADHD, as a descriptor for any slip in attention, organization, or punctuality. We laugh off minor effects and are baffled by unnamed, undiagnosed, but no less serious effects of ADHD, often blaming ourselves for the perceived inadequacies. (In a recent email apologizing for being late to a therapy session, one of my patients hit the trifecta: "OMG running late…I'm soooo ADHD LOL!")

The catch is, ADHD only affects about 10 percent of the population. Why, then, do so many people who neither have nor will ever be diagnosed with clinical ADHD think they might be affected? Perhaps, given the distractions of today's technological, device-dependent culture, many people who don't have clinical ADHD actually are more distractible and impulsive. The dependence on technology that's exploded over the last twenty years has changed how we think and behave. Our brains have literally been rewired as a result of this relatively new, tethered mode of being.

This is a condition I call Techno-ADD—it involves ADHD-like symptoms caused by technology such as smartphones and requires similar coping mechanisms as clinical ADHD. What's more, Techno-ADD affects both those with and without clinical

ADHD, because the conditions are related but are not one and the same. They're cousins rather than siblings.

Clinical ADHD has a long-standing history from before the present era of technology. It involves hereditary and biological variables and would manifest itself even if smartphones had never been invented. The two syndromes can mutually reinforce one another, without having a one-to-one correspondence. However, there is one very important thing to note for the 10 percent of us: Techno-ADD can intensify the challenges of clinical ADHD.

Because the technology that has become so much a part of our everyday lives can aggravate ADHD, it's essential for many adults both with and without clinical ADHD to develop strategies to deal with our techno-distractions. This is a critical topic to explore in the context of a book on adult ADHD today, as an experience common both to adults with ADHD and those plugged into their technology and unable to keep their attention on a single task for extended periods of time.

In other words, the question, "OMG, do I have ADHD?" is just as important as, "What do we do about it (besides LOL)?"

Someone with ADHD who is trying to focus on writing a report at work might suddenly look up and see a colleague walking down the hall, then start thinking about that person and what they might be doing. Or they might be in a Zoom meeting and suddenly get distracted by what's happening in the other participants' background. The mind quickly trails off, and it becomes difficult to pull it back to the task at hand.

Similarly, someone who is very techno-dependent may be working on a report and get a smartphone notification that someone they're following has just published a new tweet. They get pulled into checking and looking at their phone and, like their ADHD colleague, also have a hard time staying focused on their work.

To add to the chaos, the tendency to hyperfocus on the contents of our screens to the exclusion of all other cues is also common to both ADHD and Techno-ADD.

Finding ways of minimizing the distractions of technology will help anyone with either clinical ADHD or Techno-ADD, and many of the coping mechanisms will benefit both types of people as well.

It doesn't matter if you check every box of symptoms or simply feel disconnected from your sense of focus. If you're living with a sense of distraction or hyperfocus that you can't get under control—diagnosed, suspecting, or curious—the real question is what you are going to do to organize the chaos. That's what you're about to discover. Together, we're going to refocus ADHD.

ADHD AND ME: DR. DAVID SITT

My own relationship with ADHD is as personal as it is professional. I wasn't diagnosed until relatively late in life, at age twenty-two, while I was in graduate school. Somehow, I had managed to balance a thousand pages of dense reading a week across five courses, interning at a hospital, keeping my social life afloat, and teaching a full load as an adjunct professor on top of it all. That kind of workload is a lot for anyone. For me, it came with many late nights, close to the edge deadlines, and intense stress. It felt less like balancing obligations and more like constant juggling—that is, juggling ten flaming pins while walking on a tightrope wearing clown shoes over a minefield in the middle of a heavy fog.

I developed coping techniques that took advantage of my ability to hyperfocus, learned to outsource tasks, and developed systems—which you'll soon learn—to help keep me organized and on track. In this way, I successfully navigated through both college and a doctoral program in clinical psychology.

After completing my doctoral program, I threw myself into learning about my newly diagnosed condition, so as to better help myself and others. Now, in my early forties, it's easier for me to come to terms with ADHD and the circus it creates for me because I can look back on what I've accomplished. Yes, perhaps my ADHD makes me dig four holes that are ten feet deep rather than one hole that's forty feet deep, but that just means I get to wear many hats. I am a clinician, professor, entrepreneur, author, husband, and father.

I struggle with the idea that I have a "disability" or "disorder," where I'd rather use my diagnosis to better understand how my brain functions. Creativity and the ability to hyperfocus are gifts that correlate to ADHD. Those abilities are the reason I'm able to stand in a classroom of five hundred college students and deliver a creative lecture laced with humor, all while picking up the signals from everybody's facial expressions to make on-the-fly adjustments to my presentation. This constellation allowed me to jump into action when the NYC mayor's office reached out to me during COVID's second wave to help set up community-wide testing sites in Brooklyn within twenty-four hours (long story for another time). It's also how I could spontaneously propose to my wife by romantically spray-painting, "Ayla will you marry me??" outside a construction site on Fourth Avenue in Manhattan after every other plan I'd made fell through. (Joining the ranks of NYC graffiti artists was definitely a rush, and though a security guard for the construction site nearly foiled the risqué endeavor, he gave me the nod to proceed once he heard the backstory.)

ADHD has made my life difficult, but it has also made it incredible.

The definition of ADHD on a personal level varies from person to person. More than "What is ADHD," we have to ask, "What's my relationship to it? To what extent does it define who I am?"

As a father, I think a lot about my own children, particularly my seven- and five-year-old sons who have both shown probable signs of the ADHD diagnosis. Where most parents hear about the disability and the challenges, I see a complex future. I see kids who are wonderful and creative, but who will likely suffer through school and struggle to succeed if they don't figure out how to cope with and get proper treatment for it early. It's a hard thing to wrap your head around as a parent. It's even harder to process as an adult looking back over your own life if the diagnosis was missed and you struggled all the way through.

That's why it's so critical to refocus ADHD.

The first step is psychoeducation: learning what ADHD is, separating fact from projection, and seeing the upside as well as the downside. Over the years, I've enlisted the help of many other professionals who have become part of my "living with ADHD" team. There have been two psychiatrists, three psychologists, and three life coaches in total. That's aside from friends, family, and colleagues who have lent their advice and support as well. In twenty years as a therapist, I've spent thousands of hours with clients, with the privilege of becoming one of the early experts in adult ADHD. And through this book, I'm honored to join—or become the founding member of—your support team.

ADHD AND YOU: DIAGNOSIS AND TREATMENT

ADHD diagnoses have increased dramatically in recent years. However, current research believes this is not because more people now have ADHD, but because more people are recognizing and being treated for it. Yet, due to ADHD's early onset, the focus of ADHD research and literature has traditionally been on children and adolescents. Very little attention and few insights are offered for those children who enter adulthood, ADHD in tow, with all its gloom and glory.

For those adults—especially those who get a diagnosis late or not at all—it's not just resources that they lack. They often find themselves without support, understanding, and most of all, compassion.

A judgmental, unsupportive environment can impair the confidence and creativity of anyone with ADHD, from ages five to eighty-five. If you or someone you care about is diagnosed with ADHD, suspend your judgment—especially self-judgment—of the condition and uncertainty about its treatment long enough to learn that it is not a curse. There are undeniable benefits associated with ADHD, including resourcefulness and imagination.

If you allow negative emotional reactions to lead your actions, especially with children or with yourself, you may trigger the exact stigma you wish to protect them from. What's required is self-compassion, not self-judgment.

Thankfully, there is an extremely diverse toolbox of ADHD treatments to choose from along that journey, beginning with psychoeducation, as mentioned a moment ago. Coping and living more effectively involves understanding what's at the root of the challenges you're facing. Someone with ADHD needs to understand what ADHD is. What does it look like, feel like, and sound like?

There are tools for becoming more self-aware and tuned in to the present moment that can help improve functioning. These all come down to developing mindfulness—which we'll look at in depth—as an overarching philosophy of both treatment and life. We'll also draw from cognitive behavioral therapy (CBT), physical exercise, diaphragmatic breathing, and tools for time/task management, as well as medication.

Some of these will be more helpful than others, and some will be more or less helpful at different times and under different circumstances. One size does *not* fit all, and what works for you will be very personal and almost certainly change over time.

Allow time for the benefits of techniques and treatment plans to unfold. Give yourself the love and support you've always needed, and permit yourself to receive that support from others. Continue exploring the strengths and weaknesses of your brain, long after you're finished reading here. Most importantly, know this: countless people with ADHD live happy, productive lives, realize amazing achievements, and organize their chaos. You can too.

ADHD REFOCUSED: A MULTILENS PERSPECTIVE

As a professor in the department of psychology at Baruch College, part of the City University of New York (CUNY), I've taught thousands of students with varying attention levels. As a therapist, I help my patients refocus. And seeing a real and unmet need across both sets of people, I decided to write this book as a handbook to help adults with ADHD—as well as their families and friends—organize their chaos.

The book is divided into six parts, each of which contributes to another angle or lens of this comprehensive perspective. In Part I, ADHD Basics, we deal with psychoeducation, descriptively detailing the characteristics of ADHD in adulthood, the causes, and the effects. Whether you're asking yourself, "OMG, do I have ADHD?" or have already been diagnosed, Part I is meant to increase your awareness and knowledge of ADHD.

Part II, ADHD and Techno-ADD in Real Life, deals with

Techno-ADD, adult ADHD's cousin. As mentioned above, the two phenomena are different but related. If you're living with ADHD, it's almost certain that technology contributes to the challenges you're now facing, and understanding those factors will help you cope more effectively.

We'll start to dig into the adult-ADHD toolbox in Part III, Life Hacks: Behavior Change, which deals primarily with behavioral interventions. What "life hacks" will enable you to change your behavior in order to effectively meet and reduce the challenges of ADHD? Behavioral tools include the development of planning, time-management, and communication skills, as well as techniques for keeping technology—which may be threatening to take over your life—under control.

Cognitive behavioral therapy (CBT) tools take center stage in Part IV, Change Your Mind: Cognitive Tools. These include techniques for first recognizing, reframing, and changing negative, unhelpful thoughts—particularly, the recurring thought patterns that often affect those with adult ADHD.

Part V, Mindfulness: More Than a Buzzword, focuses on becoming more mindful in and of the present moment, which is the keystone to higher functioning. Mindfulness techniques are presented, discussed, and then balanced with the development of self-compassion, a vital skill for people with adult ADHD, who tend to be highly self-critical.

Because the mind and body are interdependent, Part VI, Mind Your Body, deals with body-based ADHD interventions, including exercise and conscious breathing techniques. This part also discusses ADHD medication, which can be extremely helpful when prescribed skillfully and appropriately under the care of a psychiatrist.

The 360 degrees of this handbook's circle are completed in a concluding summary of all the techniques and life hacks you'll have learned by that point. Beyond the ABCs of ADHD, we'll bring together the LMNOPs:

- L—Live your life
- M—Mindfully
- N—Noticing
- O—seeking out Opportunities
- P—creating a Personal Plan of attack

This is my 360-degree perspective and intimate knowledge of ADHD as a therapist, professor, son, husband, father, and business consultant. Together, we're going to refocus ADHD from all angles so that you can put a new lens on life.

PART I

ADHD Basics

Chapter 1

———

My Story

During my first year of graduate school at Yeshiva University, I was at the foot of the long climb toward receiving my doctorate in psychology. But it looked like I might not make it. My professor of psychopathology, Dr. Levin, had a very strict policy: "Hand in the final paper late, and you fail my course. Fail my course, and you likely fail out of graduate school."

The threat of a looming deadline typically got my engine revved and ready to go, but not before a heavy dose of expert-level procrastinating. Usually, I could calculate how much time, give or take a few hours, that I would need to complete an assignment in the day or so leading up to a deadline.

With Dr. Levin's paper, however, I miscalculated. *Really* miscalculated. At thirty pages, it was the longest paper I had ever been assigned. I needed to research and analyze over forty academic articles before even beginning to write and edit. And this was in the days *before* Google and full-text PDFs, where I actually had to pull large volumes from library shelves and photocopy each and every page.

As usual, I stayed up all night as the deadline approached, punching away at the keyboard when I wasn't staring blankly at the screen. At 9:00 a.m., the paper simply wasn't finished. It was my worst nightmare—a doomsday scenario that threatened to end my career as a psychologist before it had even begun.

Dr. Levin called me into his office. I feared he had sharpened his ax and was about to tell me, "David, you have officially splattered on the sidewalk." As I sat in front of his desk, I did everything in my power to hold it together.

What Dr. Levin said next took me completely by surprise: "Normally, such a mistake would cost you your grade, but I believe you have a serious problem that you probably aren't aware of. I believe you have Attention Deficit Hyperactivity Disorder—ADHD—and I suspect it's a strong contributor to so much of what's been challenging you in my class."

His insight hit me like a ton of bricks. It was true. I almost always arrived late to my classes, including Dr. Levin's. I was restless and often had to get up and leave the room midlecture. I struggled to focus in class, and when I did, I was in the habit of impulsively answering over and cutting off other students. And it wasn't just his class or even college—that is how my academic endeavors had always been, from first grade on.

Dr. Levin had picked up on all this and offered me an ultimatum: He would grant me an extension only if I committed to getting evaluated and treated for ADHD. Otherwise, I would fail his course and the dominoes would fall.

That's how I first learned the unmanaged three-ring circus of my life wasn't all my fault, but that I'd been battling against undiagnosed ADHD my entire life. Suffice to say I completed the paper, passed the class, and made it to graduation five years later!

EARLY BACKGROUND

As I was growing up, I don't recall ADHD being on my radar. In elementary school, back in the late '80s or early '90s, one or two of my friends were diagnosed with "ADD," but I didn't even know what it meant until that happened. When it did, I thought about their intense energy and figured it sounded right.

While my friends were bouncing off the walls, I was bouncing off my inner walls. My condition wasn't nearly as visible from the outside as it can be for other kids. I may have been fidgety, and I definitely had more doodles in my notebook than the average kid, but I was much more likely to be caught spacing out than hyping up. I certainly didn't look at the social and academic challenges I was facing, and think, "Well, that's because I have ADD like my friends do." Rather, I was riddled with a sense that I was lazier, less intelligent, and unmotivated.

Today, ADHD is the first thing a parent, teacher, or even child would probably consider when struggling in school. Back in those days, it wasn't commonly talked or thought about, and if you were diagnosed or treated, the stigma was much greater than it is now. I simply struggled through my homework and the great amount of anxiety it caused me, allowing my engine to rev up at the last minute while I finished my work at midnight from fourth or fifth grade on. Skipping over lines, missing details on math work, and struggles with writing didn't clue me in—and neither did the unconfirmed diagnoses within my own family.

Heredity, as we'll see in Chapter 3, plays the biggest role in determining the risk for ADHD, and from that standpoint, I'm probably doubly disposed to the syndrome. Several members of my family have ADHD, including my mother, while my father and sister had learning disabilities. I also grew up in the Sephardic Syrian Jewish Community in Brooklyn, which I'm convinced has a significantly higher rate of ADHD per capita than most other subsets of the general population.

Many of our community members are type-A personalities who are stimulus driven, notorious for running late (operating on "SY Time"), and don't fair too well with waiting patiently on lines. Most of the community members I've worked with who have ADHD are very good at figuring out creative ways to turn the challenges of ADHD to their advantage. They outsource a lot of what they do, are risk-takers, and are good at thinking on their feet. Many of them are quite successful within high-pressure business settings as well as in extensive community-building endeavors.

This community is both my "extended family" gene pool and the environment I grew up in, so both nature and nurture predisposed me to ADHD. It's a wonder it took me so long to be diagnosed, but as I've said, times were different then.

Without a diagnosis, I remained susceptible to distraction through high school. I struggled to achieve what it seemed others were able to do with far less effort. They'd hand in exams with ten minutes to spare, while I would only be 60 to 70 percent of the way through when the bell rang. When I took the SATs and later the GREs for grad school, I couldn't focus and sit still well enough to finish the exams in the time allotted, and my scores were barely enough to be kept in consideration of admissions. Fortunately, my creative essays and engaging interview skills (powered by the upsides of my ADHD) helped squeeze me in the doors at Baruch College (City University of New York) and later on Ferkauf Graduate School at Yeshiva University.

Today, I'd be classified as "disabled" and given extra time to finish, with a private testing environment and other accommodations to level the playing field. At that time, I didn't even know I had a so-called disability, and institutions I was in weren't as quick to provide appropriate assistance.

Like many in the ADHD community, I came up with creative life hacks in the place of real support, both to overcome *and* leverage the challenges I faced. I compensated by cultivating interpersonal skills and an emotional intelligence that helped me stand out. I did well in front of other people and in interviews. One wonderful professor, Dr. Susan Locke, who believed in me, helped me get into the honors program as an undergraduate at Baruch College, then became my mentor throughout that time—the same college where I've now taught for twenty years.

I never considered ADHD as an explanation for the all-nighters I pulled every other week or why I'd be so anxious about assignments that I would completely put them out of my mind until the due dates were hours away. It never occurred to me that ADHD was at the root of the anxiety and intermittent depression I faced while trying to keep the pace of my neurotypical friends and classmates.

I was fortunate to have developed enough out-of-the-box ways of approaching ADHD's challenges that I kept moving forward without treatment for some time—but not everyone can.

TREATMENT AND RESEARCH

After the day of reckoning with Dr. Levin in my first year of graduate school, I met with Dr. Stephen Josephson, a psychologist Dr. Levin recommended who had some experience with ADHD. This was in 2001, and the diagnostic manual at the time was the *DSM-IV*, in which the ADHD section focused almost exclusively on children.[1]

Dr. Josephson interviewed me, going over the symptoms one by one and asking if I had them. I said, "Yes, yes, yes, yes, and, *wow*, yes." It was exactly what had been happening to me since elementary school.

At the end of the interview, Dr. Josephson said, "You have ADHD, Dave. It's undeniable. Your symptoms include inattentiveness, hyperactivity, and impulsiveness."

While I knew that I liked to drive fast and was an extreme snowboarder, I now saw that I was a stimulus junkie in all areas of my life. I thrived off of high energy and high octane from anywhere I could get it—including the stress of waiting so long to start working on assignments.

I was referred to a psychiatrist, who confirmed the ADHD diagnosis and worked with me to find a medication best suited for me. Over the next few months, I tried Ritalin, Concerta, and Adderall immediate and extended release, eventually settling on Vyvanse (more on these meds in Chapter 19). With a better understanding of my brain and medication to help me cope more effectively, the three-ring circus that had overrun my life started to calm. Instead of being on a tightrope in clown shoes in the fog, I became the ringmaster directing the acts in my life. My legs were still restless, but I was now able to sit through a two-hour lecture. My capacity for focus shot up, and written projects became significantly more bearable. I finally understood the phrase "when the fog lifts."

I was also referred to a behavioral specialist, who helped me develop time- and task-management techniques over the course of that semester. I started mapping out my assignments and looking at due dates, forcing myself to start a paper a week in advance rather than the night before. I started feeling better, thinking at times that I might just be experiencing "normal" for the first time.

There was a tremendous sense of relief to have an explanation for why I had been struggling for so long. I could identify what was going on within myself. I could go to my grad school professors and explain that I had ADHD, a condition covered by the Americans with Disabilities Act, and I was eligible for accommodations to help me deal with that disability.

There was also a sense of hope. In the twenty years since I was diagnosed with ADHD, I've developed a very intimate relationship with the "disorder." Throughout the rest of grad school, I focused every assignment I could on ADHD and did my doctoral dissertation on adult ADHD. I also joined a research team at NYU under Dr. Lenard Adler that was one of the few in the country studying the syndrome in adults.

It's rare to find uncharted territory in psychology, yet there I was, at the edge of a frontier just waiting for someone to forge a new path. Amongst an overwhelming amount of research, writing, and guidance for children and adolescents with ADHD, there was little to no information for adults at that time. And I certainly wasn't the only one who needed that research and these tools. The trend was going to pick up eventually, inevitably, and I had the opportunity to be on the cutting edge of it—both for myself and as a niche for my clinical career.

Chapter 2

Adult ADHD

After my diagnosis, I knew I wanted to dive deep into the research and clinical world of adult ADHD, and I hoped to do so with the biggest names I could find. Fortunately, Dr. Edward Hallowell happened to be working in New York City, right in my backyard, leading the way in adult ADHD awareness and treatment at the Hallowell Center. As soon as I made this connection, I cold-called Dr. Hallowell and pitched myself as the ideal hire, even though there was no formal job available.

Perhaps *ideal* was a slight stretch, but I wasn't far off. My doctoral dissertation focused on adult ADHD, and my résumé included training at Lenox Hill Hospital's Center for Learning and Attention Disabilities, NYU's Child Study Center, and two years of ADHD research at NYU. The latter had involved assessing and doing neuropsychological testing on over one hundred adults with ADHD, but treatment of adults with ADHD was unchartered territory for me.

My first client as an adult ADHD clinician came from the Hallowell Center. And his circus was running full tilt. Jeremy had a vision to create an artificial intelligence bot to scour the stock market and make picks—totally cutting edge back in 2009. His ADHD brain was all over the possibilities and bringing up so many creative solutions. But he was also working a full-time job, in a relationship, and experiencing financial strain. If I'd been walking a circus tightrope, he was charming the snake, applying the clown's makeup, and selling the popcorn all at once.

All he had to do was focus on a long-term plan, and he could've launched into the stratosphere.

And all I had to do, as a brand-new young clinician, was help him get there. No big deal.

HISTORY AND BACKGROUND

English pediatrician Sir George Still first described what we now call ADHD back in 1902. In 1923, a researcher named Franklin Ebaugh discovered that brain injury in children could in some cases cause what today we call ADHD.

In 1967, the federal government started funding the National Institutes of Mental Health (NIMH) in studying the effects of stimulants on children with hyperactivity. Today, stimulants such as Ritalin and Adderall are still the most widely prescribed medication for ADHD in both children and adults.

Through the 1990s, ADHD was treated exclusively as a childhood disorder. Few stopped to think that all the children with ADHD who were being studied and evaluated during treatment should continue to be evaluated as they grew up. Even today, the study of adult ADHD continues to lag behind the progress made around childhood ADHD.

The term "ADD"—attention deficit disorder—wasn't included in the *DSM* at all until *DSM-III* came out in 1980. Previous terms used included "minimal brain dysfunction" (*DSM-I*, 1952) and "hyperkinetic reaction of childhood" (*DSM-II*, 1968). It was only in 1987 that the term "ADHD," adding hyperactivity into the mix of symptoms, formally came into use. Many people continue to use the term "ADD," since it's simpler to say.

Dates in ADHD History

	DSM-I		DSM-III		DSM-IV/DSM-IV-TR		
	"Minimal Brain Dysfunction"		"ADD with or without hyperactivity"		"ADHD: IA, H/I, Combined Subtype"		
1952	**1968**	**1980**	**1987**	**1994**	**2000**	**2013**	
	DSM-II		DSM-III-R			DSM-5	
	"Hyperkinetic Reaction of Childhood"		"ADHD, undifferentiated ADD"			"ADHD: Predominantly IA, H/I, Combined Presentation"	

The *DSM-V-TR* lists three varieties of ADHD symptoms:

- Inattention—inability to focus on mental activities, distractibility, and forgetfulness
- Hyperactivity—difficulty remaining still, fidgeting, and restlessness
- Impulsivity—taking action or speaking without thinking

These categories can present as trouble sustaining attention on tasks and conversations; taking action without thinking; difficulty waiting in lines; impulsive and verbose speech; being in constant motion (e.g., fidgeting and leg- and foot-shaking); trouble staying seated even for a short time; difficulty organizing, beginning, and finishing tasks; and losing or misplacing belongings.

Adults with ADHD are often impatient and short-tempered. They have difficulty managing their time and struggle with prioritizing and organizing day-to-day tasks. They often engage in stimulus-seeking behaviors, such as impulsive shopping, gambling, substance abuse, and arguing for the sake of arguing.

Adults with untreated ADHD impulsively "leap before they look" and are at higher risk for job loss, speeding, car accidents, drug abuse, and marital discord than the non-ADHD population.

Based on a person's unique relationship to these symptoms, the *DSM-V-TR* lists three ADHD categories or "presentation types":

- Predominantly inattentive, which includes a tendency to procrastinate
- Predominantly hyperactive/impulsive, which includes making snap decisions and inability to delay gratification
- Combined presentation, which means that both presentations are expressed

I fell into the "combined presentation" category. Many of you might immediately identify yourself, your children, or others in your life as having ADHD. Remember, however, that everyone exhibits at least a few of these behaviors at various times. What's important is the frequency and degree to which the combination of symptoms impairs your ability to function at school, work, home, or in relationships.

CURRENT RESEARCH PROGRESS

ADHD is considered a developmental disorder, meaning symptoms typically manifest before the age of twelve. Diagnosis of the condition has increased since the 1990s, as have estimates of the percentage of the population affected. However, despite claims that the syndrome is currently being overdiagnosed, it's actually not uncommon for a child with ADHD to get through school undiagnosed. In 2022, the *DSM-V-TR* estimated the prevalence of children with ADHD at 7.2 percent (up from 5 percent in the 2013 edition), although other studies indicate this rate to be an underestimation. In 2018, a National Health Interview Survey estimated a prevalence of 10.2 percent among children and adolescents aged four to seventeen, almost 1 percent greater than the Center for Disease Control's (CDC) 2013 estimate of 9.4 percent.

All of that simply means that roughly 10 percent of kids are diagnosed with ADHD, commonly between the ages of six and seventeen, and usually within the school setting. If a child isn't doing well in elementary school or high school, it will typically come to teachers' and guidance counselors' attention. As part of the process of diagnosis, a child should be screened for other problems, including learning disabilities, depression, and anxiety, which can coexist with or mimic ADHD symptoms. And any evaluation should include input from parents, teachers, and others who have regular contact with the child.

Unfortunately, while these children are treated so they can get through school, treatment often stops when they graduate or leave. And for the other kids who are never diagnosed at all, their problems often compound as life becomes more complex.

Children's highly structured support systems at home and school can often keep symptoms from boiling over, which means a growing number of adults are diagnosed with ADHD whose symptoms were overlooked during childhood. In such cases, symptoms may not only persist into adulthood but become more noticeable than they previously were. When the more unstructured environments of adulthood arrive, such as college, the workplace, and relationships, symptoms are more likely to manifest and overwhelm. Key support players' influence fades, such as parents, homeroom teachers, and therapists, adding to the adult with ADHD's emerging difficulties in self-management and executive functioning.

Up until the late 1990s, there was virtually no research into adult ADHD, with most studies focusing on children and adolescents. This is the opposite of the normal pattern in the field of psychopathology. We've learned about most psychological disorders, such as depression and anxiety, from the adults who suffer from them. Clinical and academic research into these conditions focuses on the adult population first. Only later, when it becomes apparent that children experience these conditions as well, will research then double back to include the younger as well as the older population.

By now, enough children diagnosed with ADHD have grown up under the watchful eyes of the clinicians and others treating them, building the awareness that ADHD can be a lifetime phenomenon. In fact, the disorder persists into adulthood in approximately 40 to 65 percent of cases diagnosed in childhood.[2] As such, research into adult ADHD has begun to catch up to childhood data, but still to a disproportionate degree over the past few years.

Most significantly, several longitudinal studies were published that track children who were diagnosed with ADHD twenty to forty years ago, observing their symptoms, treatments, and other variables unfold over time, compared to non-ADHD control groups.[3] I will highlight some of these findings in a later chapter.

A few reputable books have also been written about adult ADHD over the last ten years or so. Clinical psychologist Russell Barkley's book *Taking Charge of Adult ADHD* came out in 2010, followed by *When an Adult You Love has ADHD* in 2016. Psychiatrist Dr. Lenard Adler, with whom I worked at the NYU Medical School, has studied and written on the subject, as has Dr. Edward Hallowell, who now has ADHD treatment centers in four different locations across the country.

However, we're still at the early stages of understanding adult ADHD and its treatment.

MULTILENS TREATMENT

ADHD Refocused covers seven areas of ADHD management: psychoeducation, behavior modification, cognitive adaptation, mindfulness, interpersonal interactions, technology management, and a mind-body approach.

Prior to jumping into any treatments, a proper diagnosis at the hands of a well-trained mental health professional with knowledge of adult ADHD would be step one. In complicated cases, or if accommodations at work or academic settings are being considered, a more in-depth neuropsychological assessment might be warranted. With a diagnosis confirmed and motivation in place to maximize probabilities of a successful life with ADHD, the seven domains of managing your ADHD await.

Beginning with the most common approach for adults with ADHD, medication remains among the primary treatment tools, falling under the "body" category. But medication is most effective when combined with other therapeutic treatments. ADHD-informed psychotherapy and coaching are particularly important when years of personal frustration, academic and professional mishaps, and interpersonal difficulties have resulted in negative thinking patterns, low self-esteem, and debilitating anxiety. I've had many patients come to see me for depression or anxiety that turned out to be the result of untreated ADHD. Once their ADHD is properly diagnosed and treated, the depression and anxiety lessen, and a greater sense of control is regained.

My approach to treating adult ADHD integrates mindfulness-based cognitive behavior therapy into executive-function coaching. There are some basic differences between therapy and coaching that I feel make them complementary to one another. What I offer, which will be laid out in the rest of this handbook, is hybridized therapeutic coaching.

Therapy is based on the medical model: there's something out of sorts with you, emotionally, behaviorally, or otherwise, and we're here to treat or at least help you deal better with whatever that is. Patients generally go to a therapist once a week at a specified time. The therapist gives the patient advice and techniques for dealing with their problems and hopes the patient will apply them. At the next session, the therapist asks the patient how they did during the intervening week.

Coaching often takes place more frequently than therapy and is meant to serve as support throughout the week. There are more regular check-ins. You and your coach might meet over the phone for fifteen minutes three times a week. There could also be check-ins via email and text-messaging. There's a high level of accountability involved in coaching.

Coaches themselves are generally not trained in the clinical aspects of ADHD, such as dealing with the depression, anxiety, and ADHD's emotional byproducts. Nor are coaches necessarily trained in the advanced cognitive and behavioral modification techniques that are critical in treating adult ADHD.

Using those invaluable tools that I have as a therapist, I generally check in with clients more regularly than the typical therapist would, and use coaching techniques to support my work. Hence my descriptor, "therapeutic coaching."

In addition to a cognitive approach, behavioral modification techniques are important as well. People with ADHD have what is often called "time blindness," which means they have difficulty seeing beyond what's happening in the short term. They have a limited view of matters, obligations, and expectations on the distant horizon. This may sound like a description of being mindful, which we'll get into in a moment, but it's actually the opposite. It's being in the present but in a mindless and myopic way. A little blind to both the past and future.

Showing up late, missing deadlines, and disappointing people creates a lot of anxiety, guilt, shame, doubt, and fear. The cognitive techniques of CBT give us tools to explore and reflect on our thoughts and emotions, as well as to restructure our negative thinking patterns into more positive ones, while behavior modification techniques help us to beat some of those anxiety-causing issues in the first place.

Next, I've found that not just the techniques but the philosophy of mindfulness is extremely important in meeting the challenges of ADHD and living life effectively.

"Mindfulness" is a synonym for "awareness," which means mindfulness is essentially awareness training. Adults with ADHD need to develop an appreciation for their own capacity for awareness, to better notice when they're impulsive and agitated, or when they're procrastinating and distracted. Mindfulness techniques and their underlying philosophy enable adults with ADHD to downshift from autopilot and get into a more active, engaged state of mind, where they are better able to use behavioral and cognitive techniques to change what they're doing and how they're doing it. This isn't necessarily easy, so self-compassion is also crucial throughout this lifelong process.

ADHD doesn't go away. If we use these techniques regularly, we'll develop a higher level of baseline functioning. If we let go of those techniques, our ADHD will be waiting for us in full force, because it's our brain's default mode. Mindfulness is our best shot at being able to deploy behavioral and cognitive techniques when and as needed. Self-compassion is the part of the engine that keeps us going when we inevitably have tough days and mess up.

This brings us to the next piece, which is to improve the interpersonal dynamics that ADHD makes difficult. Our relationships with others, ourselves, and even our technology are all affected by ADHD. The good news is that these relationships can all be improved through specific tools as well as through mindfulness, cognitive shifts, and behavioral modification.

ADHD Refocused is less about finding out what's wrong with you and fixing it—and more about cultivating optimism, happiness, and self-compassion. There's one more piece of the psychoeducation puzzle to understand, however: how did we get this way in the first place?

Chapter 3

Clinical ADHD Causes

In graduate school, I became fascinated with the causes—what scientists call the etiology—of psychological conditions. When being trained as a clinician, we mainly explored this question in the context of pathologies, such as depression, schizophrenia, phobias, and the other maladies described by the *Diagnostic and Statistical Manual of Mental Disorders* (*DSM-V-TR*).

My clinical program didn't deal with ADHD in depth, but as it became my area of interest, I've become intensely curious about its etiology. Today, ADHD is among the top five most widely discussed mental disorders—a term that still makes me flinch when applied to ADHD.

Most disorders have little upside to them. If a person diagnosed with post-traumatic stress disorder, or obsessive-compulsive disorder, could snap a finger and get rid of the disorder, they probably would do it without thinking twice. You just want it gone. We treat and minimize disorders because we don't want to live with them at all. But there's something unique about ADHD that doesn't always feel that way. Yes, it can be dysfunctional and debilitating. Yes, there are certainly cases that we'd just like to eliminate. But not always—and not all of it.

Living with ADHD is like being on a spectrum, where we're debilitated at times and thriving in others—not just in spite of it, but because of it. Rather than thinking of it as a disorder to overcome, I like to think of it as a brain style to adapt to.

So what exactly makes our ADHD brains behave this way? It's a logical enough question, though it's not necessarily easy to answer.

NATURE: HEREDITY AND BIOLOGICAL FACTORS

Do we really know what causes ADHD? The simple, honest answer is that we don't with complete scientific certainty. But this doesn't mean we don't know anything about its origin and etiology. We actually know quite a bit.

By far the most significant influence, as far as we can tell, is heredity. Genetics play a more significant role in causing ADHD than most mental ailments, with a few exceptions, such as schizophrenia, autism spectrum disorders, and bipolar disorder.

Some studies estimate that 70 to 80 percent of the differences between people's severity of ADHD symptoms are due to genetic factors.[4] Other research suggests the number may be as high as 90 percent.[5] For perspective, these numbers are similar to genetic contributions to height, and far greater than genetic contributions to our personality traits and even IQ. Other common conditions, such as depression, generalized anxiety disorder, and social anxiety disorder, have a far lower genetic component.

Note that while ADHD has a relatively high rate of heritability, there is no single gene identified to date to be a "root cause." Rather research suggests a plethora of genes, each with varying degrees of influence, interact with environmental factors to increase the manifestation of ADHD.[6]

To dig deeper into the hereditary matrix, if one identical twin has ADHD (e.g., with a 100 percent DNA overlap), the other twin is 70 to 90 percent likely to have ADHD as well. A nontwin sibling would have a 25 to 40 percent chance of having ADHD.[7] If a parent has ADHD, research suggests that 40 to 57 percent of their children will also have it. Furthermore, 25 to 35 percent of parents of ADHD children are themselves adults with ADHD.[8] (Ready for the quiz on the next page?)

These probabilities were confirmed in my own case. Aside from me, my mother has ADHD, potentially one sibling, several nieces/nephews, and so far both my eight- and six-year-old sons are showing strong expressions of ADHD as well.

Digging further into heredity, I've also mentioned my theory that the larger gene pool I'm part of—the Sephardic Syrian Jewish community—may also be a contributing factor. And it is more than mere speculation. Our immediate families' genetic characteristics don't exist in a vacuum but are shared with our extended families and those from the same or a similar biological background.

In addition to genes, I suspect the community environment that I grew up in also contributed to my developing ADHD. But more on social and environmental factors later.

DOPAMINE AND OTHER NEUROTRANSMITTERS

The neurons in our brains and nervous system communicate through a number of different mechanisms. One of the primary ways this happens is through the transfer of chemicals known as neurotransmitters between one neuron and another. These neurotransmitters, which fulfill different communication functions, have names such as dopamine, serotonin, norepinephrine, GABA, and acetylcholine.

ADHD most prominently entails the neurotransmitter dopamine. The gene DAT1, which transports dopamine, and DRD4 and DRD5, which are dopamine receptors, appear to be specifically involved.

Dopamine is implicated in a lot of different neural and brain functions, and it is involved in our processing of rewards, pleasure, and joy. In relationship to ADHD, it plays a significant role in the brain's stimulation and reward system, because people with ADHD have a dopamine shortfall. We require more dopamine to be stimulated and to produce a pleasurable experience.

The ADHD brain underproduces dopamine, which impacts and alters the ways in which behavior is reinforced. For "neurotypical" people, as they're now sometimes called, dopamine stimulates action and reduces inhibition to taking action.[9] People with ADHD, on the other hand, require greater stimulation before they are motivated to act. For example, I waited to the last minute to write my college papers because the stress of the impending deadline was a powerful stimulant.

To bring this down to earth, say that my wife asks me to go and pick up some groceries. That's not a very stimulating activity for me. Because my brain doesn't produce the "normal" amount of dopamine, which might make me feel pleasure in doing something nice for my wife or rewarded for performing that task, I'm more likely to avoid doing it until the end of the day. What might also happen is that I'll forget to do it altogether because the immediate reward factor just isn't strong enough.

This affects my ability to plan. People are driven by what is stimulating to them, and that can involve a sense of obligation as well as pleasure. As someone with ADHD, it's harder for my brain to register any given task, such as sitting down to write a report, as genuinely important.

If I get a bill in the mail, I'll often just put it aside to deal with it later. In the battle between "now" and "not now," "not now" tends to win. Opening the bill doesn't give me the dopamine surge that would motivate many people to deal with paying it now. Out of sight, the bill may well be out of mind. It may not get paid at all, which can lead to all sorts of trouble.

Other neurotransmitters are implicated in ADHD as well, including norepinephrine, which also impacts the modulation of stimuli, that is, how the brain recognizes a stimulus. A stimulus may exist, but if it does not get recognized as such, it is ignored. Recent research is also exploring the role serotonin plays in ADHD, a neurotransmitter often implicated in depression and anxiety.[10]

When all is said and done, it simply takes more to get the attention of someone with ADHD. This is the problem that methylphenidate and amphetamine-based ADHD medications, such as Adderall and Ritalin, address.

NEUROBIOLOGY

Aside from neurotransmitter issues, we also know from brain-imaging studies that the brains of children and adults with ADHD show lower electrical activity. This is related to less blood flow and even, in some cases, less oxygen flow in certain regions of the brain.

Brain-imaging techniques have in particular found abnormal activity in the brain's frontal lobes, which, broadly speaking, involve our general capacity for paying attention—planning, organization, and working memory. The areas of the frontal lobes specifically affected are nerve fibers known as white-matter microstructures.

The analogy Dr. Russell Barkley uses in his 2017 book *When an Adult You Love Has ADHD* is to fiber-optic cables buried underground in a neighborhood.[11] Bundles of white-matter nerve-fiber microstructures enable regions of the brain to communicate more efficiently with one another, just like the bundles of fiber-optic cables buried underground make for faster web access.

In people with ADHD, these bundles are about 10 to 30 percent smaller than in neurotypicals. The smaller fiber bundles are less active and may not connect brain regions the way they do in a typical brain. This brain physiology has also been described as "cortical thinning" in the research on ADHD.[12] While such structural differences correlate with some of the deficiencies in ADHD, I often wonder if future research will show that brain differences actually account for the strengths and unique upsides of the ADHD mind.

In rare cases, brain injuries that impact normal development may play a role in the development of ADHD. It's also possible that a pregnant woman's exposing a fetus to harmful chemicals, such as lead, smoking, or alcohol, might affect the baby's auto-immune system, yielding similar results. Low birth weight might be another contributing physiological cause.

However, as far as we can tell, these are secondary and, in some cases, rare causes of ADHD. The biggest factor, again, is heredity.

NURTURE: SOCIAL AND ENVIRONMENTAL FACTORS

The age-old question of the extent to which "nature" and "nurture" influence who and what we become rises up yet again in the ADHD context. Can the childhood environment we grow up in influence the development of ADHD?

Researchers often apply the diathesis-stress model when looking at the causes of mental disorders. What this simply means is that they ask the question of whether "stresses" or environmental factors also contribute to the manifestation of illnesses, such as depression, schizophrenia, and phobias, to which there is a genetic predisposition. Do nurture and other environmental factors contribute to genes being turned on, and the condition developing, or off, with the condition remaining latent?

Even if heredity makes a contribution of anywhere from 60 to 80 percent to the development of ADHD, the lesser, remaining percentage might involve environmental considerations such as a highly stressful family situation or low socioeconomic status. Several different adverse social factors might be involved.

Familial and other environmental factors that have been studied as possibly contributing causes include:[13]

- Marital discord
- Low socioeconomic status (SES)
- Paternal criminality
- Maternal mental disorder
- Foster care placement

However, none of these factors, individual or collectively, is definitive or dominant enough to permit us to point the finger and say, "That's it. Avoid those things, and you won't get ADHD!"

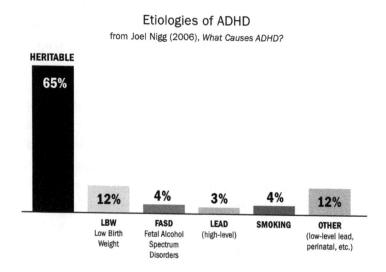

Etiologies of ADHD
from Joel Nigg (2006), *What Causes ADHD?*

HERITABLE	LBW Low Birth Weight	FASD Fetal Alcohol Spectrum Disorders	LEAD (high-level)	SMOKING	OTHER (low-level lead, perinatal, etc.)
65%	12%	4%	3%	4%	12%

When looking at the causes of ADHD, in the nature versus nurture debate, nature is certain to come out ahead. As the following chart shows, the key cause of ADHD is and is almost certain to remain heredity.

A PREVIEW OF TECHNOLOGICAL FACTORS

We've mentioned clinical ADHD's cousin Techno-ADD, which we'll soon be looking at in greater depth. However, I predict and am willing to go on record as saying that, when we look back on the research that's being conducted in the 2020s, we'll come to find that the use of technology will emerge as probably the single greatest environmental factor influencing the severity and outcome of ADHD symptoms.

A number of studies have begun to investigate the use of technology and social media's impact on ADHD. One study of children's technology use suggested that as children's screen time increased, their same-day ADHD symptoms worsened.[14] In a second study, researchers in California tracked over 2,500 high school students over a two-year period, gathering data on the types and frequency of technology and social media use, as well as tracking symptoms of ADHD. The students were screened for ADHD at baseline and were included *only* if they did not have an ADHD diagnosis up to that point in time. Remarkably, the study found a statistically significant, yet modest, association between higher frequency of digital media use and the proliferation of ADHD symptoms in the previously undiagnosed teens.[15]

Drop the mic!

While the implications here are staggering, this is one of the earliest studies to investigate the relationship between technology and ADHD, and we must wait for further research to unfold before locking in our conclusions about this potentially powerful interconnection between a purely external cause and its undeniably clinical effects.

PART II

ADHD and Techno-ADD in Real Life

Chapter 4

A Closer Look at Symptoms

Earlier today, just before sitting down to work on this chapter, I worked with an exuberant Gen-Z influencer. She has over 850K followers on Instagram, a streetwear apparel line, contracts to post stories for major brands, and four other "entrepreneurial" endeavors in the works.

She described how she often feels her mind racing, jumping around from task to task across her varied commitments, struggling to stay focused on any one thing long enough to neatly tie it up. This is a very familiar description to the ADHD adult.

While childhood descriptions include factors like "jumping over things" and "climbing excessively," adults with ADHD often are battling a constant onslaught of novel thoughts, impulsive urges, and a tendency to glance anywhere other than straight ahead. The experience is akin to being at the beach, sitting close to the crest of the ocean.

Imagine you are building a sandcastle with great focus and excitement. Suddenly a wave presses toward you and pulls you into the water. In that moment, you immediately lose sight of the sandcastle and you're occupied with being in the water.

A wave then drops you back ashore, and this time you decide to make a sand angel. A moment later the wave comes upon you, and you give in, heading back out to sea.

You're active in the water, doggy paddling, staying afloat. You briefly look up and can barely spot where you were first building the sandcastle. Then, just like that, you're back ashore at a completely different area, this time among a group of people. You interrupt their conversation and excitedly tell them about the ocean, and within what feels like a moment you're engaged in a headstand competition with your new friends...until the wave pulls you in again.

You get my drift.

Battling the constant pull of the waves takes effort, and our difficulties with sustaining attention and focus, lack of follow-through, inability to complete projects, hyperactivity, indecisiveness, procrastination, and avoidance can plague our lives and keep us from realizing our unique potential.

ADHD affects what's called "executive functioning," a loose category that includes time management, self-organization, problem solving, self-restraint, and self-motivation.

According to the *DSM-V-TR*, this can manifest in a number of ways. The inattentive type wanders off, makes careless errors, procrastinates, and is disorganized. The hyperactive/impulsive type can't delay gratification, makes decisions without considering long-term consequences, cuts off other people who are talking, and is prone to fidgeting or squirming. The combined type of ADHD exhibits both inattentive and hyperactive symptoms.

In my experience as a therapist and clinician, most adults who display hyperactive symptoms almost always display inattentive ones as well, while there are many cases of inattentiveness without hyperactivity.

In any case, let's move away from medical or technical definitions and into the subjective experience of each of these symptoms. How can we identify and name these experiences in our own lives?

INATTENTIVE

When I was in school, there were many times when I missed filling out one of the bubbles on a Scantron test. This meant that every answer afterward was incorrectly placed, and the exam would be graded incorrectly. In math, I'd often make careless errors, like not carrying numbers in long division.

Now the problem tends to be sending out emails without reading them first, texting the wrong person, or impulsively posting to social media. In school, the missed grades and extra homework those mistakes created were frustrating. Now, the stakes are much higher.

Of course, all sorts of people encounter problems like these; it's not limited to those with ADHD. But it does happen to us far more often and throughout our lives. And ADHD symptoms don't discriminate among the different parts of your life—inattention can cause trouble at work, home, school, and in relationships.

For this type of ADHD, it can be difficult to hold your attention for long periods of time, such as while listening to a talk or watching a movie. This often happens to me when I read. After a short time, I notice I didn't catch what I just read and have to go back and start from the beginning of the sentence or the paragraph. Even worse, I catch myself dozing off to sleep not long after I pick up the book (or open the page to write one!). Staying focused is an ongoing battle.

Often, someone whose spouse has ADHD will say to me, "You know, my husband is very focused when he's watching football. He catches every detail of the game and doesn't miss a call, play, or stat. But he drifts off when we're having a conversation, or when the kids ask him about schoolwork. But you can't tell me he doesn't pay attention very well when he wants to."

When someone with ADHD is stimulated and highly interested in a topic, they're certainly able to focus. One of the upsides of ADHD, in fact, is a capacity for laser-like hyperfocus when you're stimulated or elated. When you're not stimulated, however, it becomes much harder to sustain attention. This may not bode well for the spouse complaining about their distracted partner, but that's another issue for another kind of therapist.

DISORGANIZED AND DISTRACTED

The ADHD mind finds holding onto a plan of action from the beginning to the middle to the end very challenging. Again, we might say this is due to a "stimulation deficiency," which makes it hard to regulate your capacity for long-term planning.

Say you're given the task or challenge of planning a wedding. If this isn't your life's greatest dream, you'll struggle to string together the many different steps that such an involved, long-term project entails. That same struggle can happen with shorter-term projects as well, such as meal planning and then cooking dinner.

It's hard to manage sequential tasks and keep materials in the proper order. It's difficult to plan out the week, which often leads to delayed submissions, missed appointments, and a series of excuses to patch up the holes. This is frustrating both for those with ADHD and those expecting something from them.

People with ADHD are also forgetful and distracted, so they are often prone to losing or misplacing things: keys, wallet, cell phone, notes, and passwords. They forget commitments, appointments, errands, and chores. They forget to close cabinet doors and to lock the car or the garage. They might be easily distracted by external stimuli, such as people talking, and are often found putting headphones on to control the noises they hear.

Of course, we can still create fantastic experiences without being focused or organized. Sometimes our disorganization actually works out well.

A couple of summers ago, my wife and I took our then four- and two-year-old sons on a two-week trip to California, hopping down the coast from San Francisco to San Diego. We knew we wanted to go months ahead of time, but I only booked the flights ten days before we left. The only other thing I forced myself to do before the trip began was to book a car rental and the first night's hotel in SF.

We planned *everything* else on the fly.

Don't get me wrong, we loved the spontaneity of the trip. It was unbelievable. I wouldn't change a single thing about it. But not every trip works out that way, and not everyone (with or without ADHD) can pull it off. It certainly *could've* been a disaster, and I have to admit that planning just a bit more in advance couldn't have hurt.

What's more, a trip isn't the same as everyday life. I have incomplete and failed business models in my past that never got off the ground because I couldn't keep all the moving pieces going toward a cohesive business plan.

Any thought of planning out details such as what museums we would go to was so overwhelming that I couldn't even commit to booking a flight until almost the last minute. Once I committed to the flight, the trip was a reality, but 90 percent of details still remained elusive. Of course, this is just one of the many events and projects I've tackled by the seat of my pants. Over the years, my difficulty in planning and organizing have led me to delay my grad-school dissertation for a full year, renew my passport at a rush center two days before an international trip that had been booked for months, and then, there's this book…

PROCRASTINATION

Deadlines are intended to be motivating. For the average person, having a specific deadline, a certain day on the calendar, helps to create a framework of expectation. The deadline becomes a cue for planning a course of action.

This is far from what happens for me and other people with ADHD. When I saw a due date in college or grad school, I would usually just nod at it, have the "not now" thought, and then carry on to my next thought. The assignment and due date were then out of sight and out of mind.

As time unfolded, I'd move along without paying the assignment any mind. I wouldn't be anxious about the assignment because I wasn't giving it any attention. If for some reason the task or assignment popped into my consciousness, I would do a quick check at the delta from that day to the due date, and if it was more than a few days away, I would double down on the "not now" snooze move. When the assignment's deadline "suddenly" came into full view with just a few days or hours on the clock, I'd immediately feel intense anxiety about needing to get moving on the project. Those with the capacity to pull off the last-minute rush may succeed in completing the goal, reinforcing and per-petuating the last-minute habits; others may not succeed at the last-minute effort and suffer the consequences.

With my clients, I tend to use the analogy of being in a kayak heading down a river. I just glide by, enjoying the scenery, even though I'm loosely aware there are rapids ahead. But it's not until I actually hear and then see the rapids that I start paddling fever-ishly. My life now depends on it!

For better or worse, I make it past the rapids and survive 95 percent of the time. But the 5 percent of the time when I spatter against the rocks is intense and emotionally bruising.

Over the years, I've enlisted the help of many excellent professionals to help me reduce procrastinating. What's unfortunately been consistent is how difficult it is for those who don't experience ADHD to understand just how broad and deep the procrastination challenge is for me. They believe their suggestions to "just do it" or "just get started" certainly would work if I "just" followed such advice. But that's not so simple with an ADHD brain. It would be like asking someone who wears glasses to just "squint harder" to see.

I've told many of my clients that I face the same problems they do. I can move into a new home on short notice but leave a few boxes unpacked for six months or more. I can refurnish a room on a whim but never get all the final details into place. I'll often write an article I think has a lot to offer but will stop short of publishing or posting it.

Why would we put all this effort out and then stop or even sabotage ourselves before a project reaches completion? Could this be due to fear of criticism or judgment? Is it a battle with perfectionism?

I've found there are more nuances here than first meet the eye. People with ADHD have an aversion to the tedious details that are often the last steps in tying up large projects—putting the proverbial stamp on the envelope. Final steps are often devoid of the creative flare and energy boost that come with working through an endeavor's core steps.

This could also be why so many of my blog entries fade before I finish them. Enthusiasm dwindles and the gusto of a good idea becomes harder to sustain when writing begins to become more arduous.

HYPERACTIVITY AND RESTLESSNESS

The other main ADHD category or silo involves hyperactivity and impulsivity. For some with ADHD, there's a propensity to have a lot of physical energy and to be very fidgety. When I was in school, those in back of or in front of me would get very irritated because I couldn't stop clicking my pen, shaking or crossing my legs, and tapping their chairs.

People with ADHD have a hard time staying seated for long periods. They have to get up and move around.

When I was in elementary school, the rule was "You can't get up out of your chair unless you have to go to the bathroom." I went to the bathroom three times a period, in every class. I would tear out pages from my notebook and crumple them up just to have an excuse to walk over to the trash bin. I desperately needed to get up and get my "wiggles" out.

This sense of restlessness can become pervasive. When I'm at home with my wife and we're both reading, she reads quietly, while I burst out with a comment every other paragraph. It's not easy for me to sit quietly and just read, so I temper my hyperactivity with impulsive conversation. "Oh my god, you have to hear what I just read about. I just learned the most amazing thing. Whoa, listen to this quote! Have you ever wondered about this?" Suffice to say, such impulsivity can wear down those on the ADHD adult's periphery.

The *DSM-V-TR* describes people with ADHD as being driven by a motor. This references the perpetual mental and at times physical momentum that those with the hyperactive/impulsive tendencies typically experience. Imagine a top that spins and spins, often in a wobbly manner, with barely any downtime to recalibrate. Similarly, those with ADHD can be verbose and talk both more often and faster than others, with speech that often feels pressured. Unfortunately, the inefficiencies of redirecting or even stopping such momentum complicates matters further. It would be like driving a Tesla (0 to 60 in 2.3 secs) with Fiat breaks (an update to Dr. Hallowell's famously quoted Ferrari/Chevrolet mashup).

IMPULSIVITY

People with hyperactive/impulsive ADHD can't wait. They can't wait in lines because waiting is more painful than having their fingernails pulled out. When I go to a movie theater or even Costco, I jockey from one line to the next, gauging which might be moving faster. It kills me if the line next to me moves faster than the one I'm in. I might even change lanes three times just to avoid the possibility of waiting one minute longer than I need to.

When I watch a movie or a TV show, I frequently give a running commentary that's very irritating to the people around me. This can be one of the most prominent impulsivity symptoms of ADHD. You're constantly interrupting other people in the middle of conversations and can't let them finish their sentences.

People with hyperactive/impulsive manifestations of ADHD are the ones who burst out with an answer before the teacher finishes asking a question. They interrupt whoever is running a meeting. If they walk over to a group of people by the coffee station, they just burst out with a comment, rather than saying, "Excuse me, can I ask you a question?" They don't have the patience to wait for an opening; they make an opening by forcing themselves in.

This same propensity is what leads people with ADHD to drive recklessly and as fast as they can. They're more inclined to get traffic violations because they speed and run red lights. Either they're not paying attention, or they don't have the patience to deal with rules that slow them down. As you can well imagine, this often leads to trouble.

Living with ADHD means frequently battling the urge to take impulsive action. Planning things out would mean delaying gratification, and that frustration often leads to impulsive purchases and buying. On Amazon's Prime Day, people with ADHD have much bigger shopping carts than their non-ADHD counterparts. They are prone to impulse buying. They go to a store to buy one item and walk out with six.

By the same token, people with ADHD can be highly indecisive. They find it difficult to make choices and decisions, because that would mean committing to a plan, and they have trouble planning.

When I leave my office to go to lunch, it can take me several minutes of pondering just to decide which restaurant to go to—even though I make the same basic decision every day. When I walk down the cereal aisle, I'm overwhelmed and often frozen with indecisiveness. I often avoid situations where I have to decide among many different options. In part, this is because people with ADHD have a high propensity for perfectionism. There's a sense that I need to get it just right, because getting it right is stimulating, and getting it wrong is devastating.

THE BIG DOWNSIDE: LIFE SPAN

In early 2018, I attended a national ADHD conference (APSARD. org) where the leading researchers and clinicians in the field gathered to discuss their latest findings and explore treatment innovations. I had a chance to catch up with several of the bigwigs I worked with while doing research just after grad school, including Russell Barkley, the ADHD Jedi Master.

Barkley's talk at the conference delivered some very startling and sobering news. He had been investigating the impact of ADHD on estimated life expectancy. Having crunched the initial data just ten days prior to the conference, he reported that those with ADHD are liable to live anywhere from ten to twenty years less than those without, depending on the severity of their syndromes.

Those with ADHD are prone to many longevity risk factors, including car accidents, substance abuse, hazardous activities such as extreme sports, marital discord, incarceration, stress, anxiety, and depressive disorders, among many others. All these factors in combination increase stress levels, impact overall well-being, and thereby ultimately reduce life expectancy.

While Dr. Barkley warned that these findings were very preliminary, they nevertheless had an alarming impact.

Since then, Barkley and others have published their findings, which indeed support his initial impressions, albeit with slight variations to exact life expectancy numbers. Barkley's study showed a 13 percent reduction in life expectancy for children whose ADHD persists into adulthood, with a nine- to twelve-year reduction in life expectancy for young adults.[16]

That represents more loss of life than obesity, poor nutrition, smoking, and alcohol use combined. For children growing up with ADHD and not receiving treatment, the condition persisted until adulthood with an even greater reduction in life expectancy.

Another analysis phrases it this way: "Originally considered a childhood-onset persistent disorder, recent evidence demonstrates that adolescent- or adult-onset of ADHD symptoms that follow volatile trajectories across time are common and associated with adverse health and social outcomes."[17]

The good news is, it's always possible to rise to the challenges of ADHD through treatment. And it looks like your life—in quality and in actual years—may depend on it.

Chapter 5

Emotional Byproducts of ADHD

In my work with clients, I often find issues not covered in the official *DSM-V* criteria to be relevant to their experience of ADHD—namely, the range of emotional dysregulation and byproducts that manifest for them. So let's consider how the emotional side of ADHD plays out, both on a diagnostic level and in everyday life.

EMOTIONAL DYSREGULATION

The unspoken symptom of ADHD, at least in terms of what is not enumerated in the current *DSM*, is emotional dysregulation. There is an inability to regulate anxiety, depression, frustration, and anger adequately—in a way that takes us from zero to one hundred in a moment. Disproportionate amounts of emotion can come to bear in a heartbeat, then just as quickly drop right back down again.

People with ADHD, especially those with hyperactive/impulsive manifestations, have a shorter frustration tolerance. They're more likely to get worked up, feel anxious, and experience depression. And, on the positive side, they're often passionate and gregarious people who have higher energy levels than most.

Not everyone experiences their emotions in this way. Similarly, while not all emotional disorders—such as anxiety and depression—are connected to ADHD, ADHD often leads to or intertwines with the symptoms of these disorders.

Just recently, a new client came to me hoping to address years of stress, depression, and high levels of anxiety. Soon into our conversation, it became clear that the symptoms that were clearest to him were connected to a long history of procrastination and inattentiveness that likely stemmed from ADHD. However, because he had done well in school, with an undergraduate degree from a reputable university, then a master's degree after that, he had never considered ADHD as a possibility until we started to look at it together.

Even the clients who show up with 90 percent confidence that they have ADHD often have some other nuance to untangle that only an outside perspective can really identify. They may have had a diagnosis already or have just done a lot of research, and we do work to confirm it before moving on—but in some cases, there's more to uncover. Maybe some generalized anxiety has gone unaddressed, or something new has emerged in the years since their diagnosis.

Sometimes those first appointments look like someone scratching their head about why life feels so hard, without any idea where to begin. Other times they have past diagnoses, long-term coping mechanisms, and internal stories about what they're dealing with.

Think about these conversations like we're trying to identify a monster. I don't mean a scary *Stranger Things* monster, but more of a semi-silly, potentially disruptive *Monster's Inc.* or Muppets type. The person shows up with a wiggling, giggling, growling, sometimes toothy bag of fur and monster parts, sets it on my desk, and asks me how in the world they can begin to tame it.

Sometimes, when the fur is flying, it can look a lot like we've got an ADHD monster—but once we get to know it, the details become clear, and we can see that it's actually an anxiety gremlin. And if you try to tame anxiety like it's ADHD (or vice versa), you might be in trouble out in creature land. This is the problem with misdiagnosis.

When we get the ADHD or other monster named right, we can't stop there. What if another fuzzy leg or random horn pops out? If there are actually *two* creatures to deal with and you only see one, you can put all of the energy you want toward one and still miss a significant part of your care. Comorbidities, like the ADHD monster partnering up with a depression goblin, are vital to untangle in order to address the disruptions fully.

And that's not all! There are also byproducts of ADHD, which is when the ADHD monster sprouts a little wart or an extra horn. Sometimes those byproducts can hit enough of a crescendo that they coalesce into their own, coexisting condition. What started off as "just" ADHD is now a two-headed monster that needs to be approached with its own sort of consideration.

In all of these cases, seeing the byproducts of ADHD, its potential misdiagnosis, and the comorbid conditions that may live alongside it *through the lens of ADHD*—regardless of whether it feels like a wart or a whole other creature—can help us better address the circumstances that caused you to seek help in the first place.

DIAGNOSIS AND MISDIAGNOSIS

ADHD can look like many other conditions. Not only do the symptoms mirror other conditions, but there's a lot of "comorbidity" to consider—an overlapping of other conditions alongside ADHD. Often, only a mental health professional can tease out the differences between ADHD and what might be an altogether different condition—the other monster in the room.

Let's take a simple example of misdiagnosis. Someone with significant sleep difficulties might experience several nights of insomnia, making it hard for them to focus their attention. They may start making or feel like they're making careless mistakes. They're easily distracted by external stimuli and may become more impulsive and irritable. These are all symptoms that look very much like ADHD, but it's possible that this person's insomnia and resulting cognitive impact are short-term, circumscribed problems. ADHD, on the other hand, is a developmental disorder that occurs and needs to be addressed over a long time span—often a lifetime.

Generalized anxiety disorder (GAD) is another common misattribution for ADHD. According to the *DSM-V-TR*, those with GAD experience excessive anxiety and worry (apprehensive expectation) across multiple domains of their life, with difficulty controlling the worry. In addition, they may experience restlessness, difficulty concentrating, irritability, fatigue, muscle tension, and disturbances in sleep. This basically describes nearly all of my ADHD clients! The nuanced difference is that for those with ADHD, the "generalized worry" is typically generated by their ADHDisms, and their anticipatory anxiety revolves around their tasks and procrastination battles. For those with ADHD, when they are in a good groove of focus and productivity, or even if on vacation, their anxiety tends to temporarily diminish. Unfortunately for those with GAD, the anxiety is pervasive and does not ebb and flow.

Several of the symptoms of depression can also mimic the ADHD experience: difficulty concentrating and sustaining attention, being absent-minded or forgetful, becoming distracted by internal emotional stimuli, and for some, being prone to negative thinking patterns and potentially hopelessness. However, even if the symptoms of depression are spread out over, say, a two-week or even two-year period, they may not manifest themselves consistently over the past fifteen years of your life, as ADHD generally does. In such cases, ADHD is not the underlying problem.

Another diagnostic challenge is differentiating between ADHD and bipolar disorder. The hyperactivity and impulsivity of ADHD, especially when severe, can be misattributed as bipolar disorder's mania and/or hypomania if not adequately understood. Likewise, the common byproduct of depressive bouts of ADHD might be misattributed to the depressive arm of bipolar disorder. Diminished ability to concentrate and indecisiveness are aspects of both conditions as well. Note that this is an oversimplification of the diagnostic challenges of differentiating the two conditions, and to adequately do so would require the consultation of a trained mental health professional with knowledge of each.

An important quality when differentiating ADHD is the fact that it is a development syndrome, as mentioned in Chapter 2. This means that symptoms emerge in childhood to teen years, even if a formal diagnosis is missed until adulthood. While the *DSM-IV* held that ADHD asserts itself no later than age seven, the *DSM-V* increased that limit, saying it has to be developmentally present by the age of twelve. Now, research has begun to present findings of initial symptom onset up to seventeen years old. A few recent studies have gone so far to suggest that bona fide ADHD can manifest in adulthood without any prior symptoms in childhood.[18] The latter assertion of adult-onset ADHD is a major divergence of the long-held developmental views and is not likely to become a dominant view.

While keeping these variances in mind, the diagnosis process makes the onset of symptoms a key consideration in figuring out whether ADHD is the root cause of a person's functional impairment. If you have ADHD, our current understanding is that your condition is chronic and has been with you most of your life—which is quite different from the way such syndromes as anxiety and depression generally manifest. Panic attacks, for instance, may come and go, but ADHD is unremitting and ever present, even if the level of impairment fluctuates.

You can begin to see how difficult it is to identify and correctly diagnose—let alone properly treat—adult ADHD. Now let's consider what happens when other concerns are stacked on top of it.

COMORBIDITY

Half of all the people with ADHD also suffer from comorbid (i.e., co-occurring) conditions—the two-headed monster we talked about earlier. This most prominently includes anxiety disorders and mood disorders such as depression and bipolar disorder. About 15 percent also have substance abuse problems. At times these co-occurring conditions exist independent of one's ADHD, and at times they branch out very much from one's ADHD.

This can get confusing sometimes, because common byproducts of ADHD, alongside emotional dysregulation, include feelings of frustration and anxiousness brought on by the struggles we face when interacting with the rest of the world. Day-to-day missteps that occur with ADHD can include missed deadlines; relationship struggles; job difficulties, including getting fired; and losing money—all of which can cause moments, days, and even weeks of sadness, for example. These are the warts or byproducts that often pop up all over our ADHD monster.

But it's helpful to know that the warts can sprout into a second head of the monster, enough to become their own condition worth treating. This would be the difference between something like "normal" sadness, so-called subclinical depression, and clinical depression. Normal sadness can be an emotional byproduct of ADHD that treatment can resolve; clinical depression is a comorbid condition that needs its own focus.

A clinical or major depressive disorder occurs when the symptoms of depression are experienced for a minimum of two weeks. These include intense sadness, recurring negative thoughts, hopelessness, sleep disturbances, crying, and low energy levels, among others. It is not uncommon for people to experience one or more of these symptoms from time to time, without them lasting two weeks.

Let's leave the monsters for a minute and go back to our ocean analogy for this one. Suppose you're on the beach just as the water's edge, and you step onto the wet sand to see a small hole form. When the water rushes in, it will fill up that hole and quickly return it to normal. The larger the hole, the longer it will take for the tide to return it to normal. And if you're stuck down in a five-foot hole, waiting for it to level back off, the water rushing in to fill it will create a very different experience than when it just washes over your feet on the shoreline. It can feel a lot like drowning, with no end in sight.

These are the different levels of depression that, while one isn't any less real than the other, require very different diagnosing and treatment approaches. What's important to realize is that, if ADHD is the underlying trigger of one's depression, treating the depression alone is insufficient. Looking primarily through the lens of ADHD can help one approach the depression more effectively, since the two are interconnected.

Anxiety is another common comorbidity for people with ADHD, part and parcel with the frustrations of having to figure out how to manage one's schedule, time, energy, and commitments. It's anxiety provoking to not be proficient at these things, and to top it all off, people with ADHD have a strong perfectionistic drive that may result in general anxiety and, in some cases, may lead to panic attacks.

Both depression and anxiety that stem from underlying ADHD can be marked by irrational belief systems that distort the interpretation of one's environment. Say, for instance, you're at a job interview where the interviewer isn't making good eye contact. You might conclude—for no good reason—that this is because you're not likable and therefore won't get this *or any other* job. You're hopeless! Such irrational interpretations can be tied to events and setbacks that might happen to anybody, such as getting a parking ticket, not getting asked on a second date, or being passed up for a job opportunity.

When your experience of the adult world is shaped by these irrational interpretations, a drive for perfection, and a tangled mess of emotions, it's difficult to know that it's not "just you," much less pinpoint the exact cause. People often seek treatment for anxiety and depression—as well as insomnia, substance abuse, relationship turmoil, and other emotional and cognitive disorders—without realizing that undiagnosed ADHD is a major underlying variable.

However, if you learn, through proper assessment and evaluation, that ADHD is the actual underlying cause, you can give it proper attention and treatment, which will also give you the tools you need to better modulate the comorbid symptoms such as anxiety, depression, guilt, and shame.

LIVING WITH ADHD'S EMOTIONAL BYPRODUCTS

Now that we have a better idea of the monster arena that is ADHD, we can get back to the focus of this chapter: the emotional byproducts that can arise even if you aren't diagnosed with clinical comorbidities that mask or exacerbate your ADHD.

Struggles with procrastination, time management, and getting organized leave adults with ADHD with near constant difficulties in work, school, home, and relationship settings. Pushing work to the last minute—even when, as is not uncommon, the results are top-level—means stress levels are often high. Missed deadlines and instability are often coupled with frustration and a lack of self-compassion.

Often, the "inner critic" is fundamental to the self-image of people with ADHD, and a treatment approach that ignores this facet is bound to fall short.

One client of mine, a young man in his late twenties, came to me with undiagnosed ADHD around the time he'd reached grad school. He was incredibly smart and had made it through high school and an Ivy League university, but the lack of structure in grad school presented a problem. He was completely overwhelmed by the fifty-page writing assignments on his plate and had begun to slip into avoidance in order to cope. When we spoke, he was on the verge of failing the semester and in quite a funk about how ineffective and worthless he felt. The closer he got to failing, the more embarrassed and depressed he became, and by that point his young marriage was starting to suffer as well.

When I saw the underlying ADHD, including a history of procrastination that had slipped under the radar in his earlier years in school, we started to work on his executive-functioning skills. We brought in some structure and an organized approach to his overdue projects. We broke everything down into smaller parts. We found a planner system for him and developed methods of accountability, both to me and to his spouse. We brought in meditation, as well as some cognitive therapy tools.

As he started to tackle his projects, one by one, his mood began to lift as well. Over eight months working together, he completed all of his courses and pulled through to the other side of depression.

Six months after we took a break from working together, I got a phone call from that same young man. He had landed a research-based job but had begun to feel funky again. The medication he'd been prescribed had helped him for a time, but it wasn't enough on its own. Together, we dusted off the toolbox and helped him find his footing again, and the depression—as a byproduct of ADHD—once again began to lift.

Contrast this with someone who has a primary, comorbid case of clinical depression—such as a woman I worked with who was building an organic snacks business as a second career. She made it all the way through to the launch but found herself in such severe depression that she couldn't get out of bed. She was isolated from her friends, gaining weight, and beginning to have suicidal thoughts.

She also had severe symptoms of ADHD that left her disorganized and frequently procrastinating. But the depression had such a strong grip on her mind and self-perception that she couldn't even give herself a shot at trying something new. Before we could work on her depression, she had to see a psychiatrist who would take an aggressive stance in treating her depression. The tools we added focused on mindfulness and cognitive therapy specifically for the depression, and only after we made some headway did we start to implement tools to help her with ADHD.

For both clients, the ultimate result was a feeling of worth and capability. But each needed to follow their own path based on their primary concern and most pressing roadblocks between them and the skills and tools they needed to thrive before the emotional byproducts could be fully addressed.

TREATMENT AND MODULATION

As a therapist, I begin treating someone whose root condition is ADHD by giving them the tools to improve their day-to-day functioning—tools we'll be going over in detail in the treatment sections later on—to better guard against the byproducts that stem from day-to-day frustrations. At the same time, I'll give these people techniques to combat their existing depressive-thinking or anxiety patterns.

The overall approach is to enable the patient to realize that, if they're putting effort into treating ADHD, they'll see a reduction in their anxiety and depression as well.

If you use behavioral-management, mindfulness, and cognitive-therapy tools to tackle ADHD, you can institute a robust treatment for both the underlying cause *and* any comorbid conditions. This is in contrast to treating such symptoms as depression without treating the underlying ADHD—an approach that will be far less effective against depression or anxiety connected to ADHD.

However, there are also cases when a patient comes in with ADHD and depression or anxiety that are really independent of one another, meaning their depression or anxiety exists alongside of but not as a direct byproduct of ADHD. In such cases, as a clinician, I have to determine which of the conditions—ADHD, depression, or anxiety—is more severely disabling in the person's life. Whichever condition is more functionally impairing is then treated first.

For example, if someone with ADHD has clinical depression so severe that they're not getting out of bed, haven't gone to work, or are suicidal, that depression must be the first thing to be treated. Once they are more functional, our focus can expand to dealing with ADHD as well. Similarly, obsessive-compulsive disorder (OCD), social anxiety, health anxiety, phobias, PTSD, and other presenting comorbidities will often need to be dealt with first and primarily if that's a patient's dominant condition at the time they come in for treatment.

ADHD is generally a lifelong condition, with both core difficulties and associated conditions that constantly recycle. You may struggle to maintain your vitality at work, school, and home to varying degrees throughout your life. Fortunately, knowing there are steps you can take to alleviate some of the pressure of the syndrome can keep that weight from crushing you, and a mindful overarching philosophy about your ADHD can allow you to be more forgiving of yourself, accepting of your ADHD, and better equipped to navigate your life and relationships.

Chapter 6

———

Relationship Challenges

If you have ADHD, it's impossible to be in a relationship where the condition doesn't have a significant impact on your partner, both day-to-day and in the long run.

However, it's frustrating enough to struggle with time management, organization tasks, physical space, and bringing our impulsive tendencies under control. To then be mindful of the impacts on your partner, family members, friends, and coworkers is a mega-challenge that seems impossible to overcome.

Furthermore, anyone in a relationship with someone with ADHD will experience their own flavor of frustration, at times even more intensely. While every relationship in our lives can be affected in some way by ADHD, the focus here will naturally be on relationships between significant others—romantic partnerships, life partnerships, and marriages. These are our closest relationships with the most frequent interaction, which means they require the most work.

THE ROLE OF YOUR SIGNIFICANT OTHER

I'd venture to say that features of ADHD may have been what attracted your romantic partner to you. They may have been drawn to your exuberance, excitement, and passion, and they may have enjoyed your hyperfocus on them in the early stages of your relationship. Your spontaneity and energy felt like a rush, or a breath of fresh air—so much that they may have overlooked the fact that you ran a little late picking them up for most dates or that you often interrupt them while they are talking. They didn't realize that your ADHD is the reason you forgot to purchase tickets to the play you were going to see on your first anniversary, even if the ensuing spontaneous Uber tour of your best date spots turned out to be a blast.

But time passes, and as with all romantic relationships, the glow wears off. The challenges of ADHD become more prominent, and the true, full picture of your relationship with each other emerges.

One partner may have good time-management skills, but both members of the couple have schedules they're trying to maintain—social obligations, children's schedules, and so on. Frustration arises for the neurotypical partner when the ADHD partner continually mismanages time, sometimes leading to the family running late or missing events altogether.

And time management is far from the only issue. I have a client who's the CTO of a major tech company. His wife of three years complains that he's constantly distracted by and hyperfocused on work. He's tethered to the phone. There isn't a conversation that goes by where my client's eyes aren't darting back and forth between his phone and his partner, barely making eye contact with her. The distraction has come to the point where the wife is threatening to leave the relationship.

These sessions came about because, in my practice, I inform every client that they should strongly consider inviting their life partner—their spouse, their boyfriend, their girlfriend, or who-ever—at some point in our work together, to attend at least one or two meetings. We can then hear that person's perspective, which gives the partner with ADHD insight into how their condition challenges that significant other. I would say that 90 percent of the time this is an eye-opening experience for both individuals, and it has long-lasting, positive effects.

To truly maximize a relationship with someone with ADHD is to get involved with and understand their condition. This does not mean becoming the partner's therapist or coach, or expecting that level of support from your partner, of course. In any relationship, it's unhealthy to take on too much responsibility and ownership of a partner's difficulties. The appropriate role to embody or expect is simply as cheerleader and support mechanism.

When your partner can serve as a feedback loop or mirror, you can better gauge where you're at with your symptoms, which helps you decide which tool to pull from the toolbox or when to consider changing medication. Such collaboration inevitably leads to healthier relationships.

COMMUNICATION, EMPATHY, AND FRUSTRATION TOLERANCE

Communication is the foundation of any close relationship—and communication with hyperactive, impulsive ADHD partners can be especially challenging. It can be hard to connect with someone whose speech is rapid or who tends to cut their partner off, not letting them finish their sentences. When inattention is part of the ADHD mix, difficulties of sustained focus, procrastinating on important conversations, and spotty follow through are just a few elements that can contribute to an eroding relationship dynamic. Without a steady dose of empathy going *both* ways, navigating these dynamics can be arduous and risk erosion of the relationship's seal.

When times get tense and the chips are on the table, people with ADHD-based emotional dysregulation also tend to have low frustration tolerance. Because we crave stimulation, we often get into fights easily, and thrust deep wounds due to poor filtering and impulse control. A simple disagreement about who left the basement light on can quickly devolve into accusations about fiscal irresponsibility and threats of sleeping on the couch.

Furthermore, the ADHD individual's propensity toward rejection sensitivity can yield a jagged emotional battlefield. Rejection sensitivity, also referred to as rejection sensitivity dysphoria (RSD), is the tendency for some with ADHD to react in extreme ways to the slightest whiff of actual or perceived rejection, criticism, or teasing. Such incidents can be triggered within moments of feeling turned away or rejected, and the RSD response can play out as rage, extreme depression, withdrawal, and/or intense self and other criticism.

The intensity of such "wounds" are described by those with RSD as unbearable, devastating, and akin to feeling punched in the gut. In this way, those with RSD process such interactions in ways beyond a neurotypical as well as others with ADHD who do not experience RSD. For example, a couple I work with is expecting a newborn in the coming weeks, and during one of our sessions Albert, the non-ADHD spouse, commented that they hadn't gotten around to buying a crib yet. At that point, Penny, the spouse with ADHD, launched into a tirade. "I can't handle everything! I told you I wanted a white crib and that my sister might give us her old one. Why are you giving me a hard time about this?" Albert tried to explain that he was not criticizing Penny but was just pointing out that the crib was something they were still working on. After several minutes of processing, Penny acknowledged that she felt attacked and criticized and reacted in haste. Such interactions are not uncommon and require people to make a concerted effort to become more mindful and to develop skills to help reduce the impacts of RSD.

For both partners, learning how to engage in reflective listening can help in these areas. After hearing the other person speak, and before answering with your opinion, reflect back what you heard: "I think I heard you say a, b, c, and that made you feel x, y, z, and led you to behave in this or that way. Did I hear you correctly?"

For example, "I think I heard you say that I was very rude to your parents at dinner, and that made you feel angry, frustrated, and like you wanted to dig a hole in the sand out of embarrassment. Did I hear you correctly?"

If the person who originally spoke feels that there was a miscommunication, they might say, "Well, you're correct about x and y, but what I really meant when I said z was the following." This gives the opportunity for clarification, and the conversation can proceed along similar lines.

This slowed-down process can sometimes feel clinical. But it greatly enhances information flow and makes it more probable that each person is hearing the other and not just reacting based on their own internal dialogue.

CONVERSATIONS AND ADHD

Being engaged in conversation with someone who has ADHD can be quite the roller-coaster ride. For the person who has ADHD, it's not any less confusing. As you start off in the conversation, you're stimulated by listening. Within moments and without warning, your mind starts to drift. You want to listen, so you have to tell yourself to "focus, focus" to get back on point. Suddenly, there's a distraction and you lose focus again. Then, when the person talking gets to the finish line, you tune back in and have to ask, "Wait a minute, can you repeat that?"

TRYING TO LISTEN WHEN YOUR PARTNER IS TELLING A STORY

START — DRAMA — FINISH

COOL! HMM... FOCUS! FOCUS! OMG! WAIT, IS THAT A SPIDER? WHOA! WAIT... CAN YOU REPEAT THAT?

I was on the train the other day with my wife, and she was telling me about something that happened at work. I *was* listening, but my ADHD brain processes fourteen tracks of thought or stimuli at once. Someone on the train had an interesting walking stick and another gentleman had obviously spent months cultivating a remarkable mustache and beard.

Now, in my mind, I still heard (nearly) every word my wife was saying. But her experience was that I was focused on other things and not listening. She told me she was going to stop talking, and I objected that I was actually listening to what she was saying, even if it seemed otherwise. In fact, in that instance, I was able to reflect back nearly word for word what she had said. But there have been many other times where I lost at that game and realized I hadn't heard quite as much as I thought I did.

The less mental training and fewer tools you have for improving awareness and observing both your inner and outer experiences, the harder it will be to control the flow of your mind in such a scenario. This can become a real problem in your relationships, but it's a problem that can be addressed and improved with committed effort.

EMPATHY BETWEEN PARTNERS

The need for empathy when ADHD is a factor is fundamentally no different than it would be in any relationship. But because ADHD relationships are more prone to disagreement, arguments, rejection sensitivity, and frustration, empathy does become paramount. It's crucial that both parties cultivate it.

One way of doing this is to educate yourselves to better understand ADHD. Read articles, listen to online talks, attend a seminar together, or, if necessary, go to therapy together. The partner with ADHD is not intentionally trying to create frustration—whatever feels problematic is actually part of a much broader picture.

Growing up, I was able to witness this dynamic at work firsthand with my parents. My mother has ADHD, and my father was the polar opposite of ADHD (e.g., methodically organized, always early, a one-track thinker). Before he passed, my father liked to travel early in the morning. They were "snowbirds" who always went to Florida for the winter, and while he was organized, packed, and ready to go first thing, my mother would make a taxi wait fifteen minutes because she forgot her makeup. Such ADHDisms frustrated my father, and his extremely organized rigidity frustrated my mother as well.

While I think my diagnosis at age twenty-two came somewhat late, she wasn't evaluated until she was in her midsixties. The diagnosis explained a lot of the frustration my father had felt with her for so many years. They dealt with their struggles by simply toughing it out and persevering. They let off steam with other people.

After she was diagnosed, she was prescribed medication, and knowing the root cause of their frustrations gave them a new perspective.

But education alone doesn't change things—it's the empathy that we cultivate from that education that makes a difference. In my parents' old-school, traditional, conservative background, knowing was never quite enough. My mother still had emotional and organizational struggles, and my father was still frustrated by them.

Even so, more often than not, people with ADHD end up gravitating toward people who complement them and provide the structure they lack. As with my parents, I know countless cases where a disorganized, time-blind, impulsive individual is married to one who is type-A, highly organized, very structured, and maybe a bit rigid.

In my clinical practice, I rarely see a case where both members of a couple have ADHD, though it certainly happens and presents exponential challenges when it does. If both partners are tuned into their ADHD and actively work on their symptom management, mindfulness, and communication skills, the familiar experience can be cementing rather than explosive.

FINDING YOUR OWN BALANCE

My wife, Ayla, and I started dating in 2010—though technically we had first met the year before. She was enrolled as a post baccalaureate (e.g. second degree) in my Intro to Psychology class of 450 students, and without me knowing it, she had developed a bit of a crush. Months after the semester ended, she sent me a message on Facebook to ask if I'd like to meet up. She wasn't a current student, which made my strict boundaries a little bit fuzzy, but I still didn't want to cross them. So I pushed her off and pushed her off, until finally I decided we could simply meet to discuss psychology.

Over coffee, I found that she graduated from college four years prior, had already worked in finance, then lost her job in the 2008 crisis and thus returned to school to shift to the medical field. My class was the psychology course she needed to keep going—not at all the young adult just entering the world that I usually taught.

What wasn't supposed to be a date absolutely turned into one. We hit it off, and that was that. A decade later, we are happily married with four children and plenty of frustrations that stem from my ADHD and her lack thereof.

Like my parents, I run late when she's ready and waiting to go. The urgency of leaving triggers a hyperfocus state that makes me see all of the things we need to do before leaving, and taking care of such "must dos" takes up the time I'd needed to get ready.

Since Ayla has highlighted this tendency as a major frustration point, I continually strive to get ahead of this by making a list in my mind, or on paper or my phone if it's a "big" departure such as a day trip or weekend away. Reviewing the list thirty minutes, then fifteen, then five minutes before our intended departure time significantly helps reduce my last-minute boggles.

But Ayla has also taken steps to be more understanding of my two-minute dash back in the house after all the kids are buckled in the car. The same hyperfocus that led me to take her out four times the first week we were dating is also what helps (or rather forces) me to notice important hanging chads when it's time to leave—such as lights left on, the baby's bottle that was left in the kitchen, and the open window in the back bedroom.

Another frustration point we've found is in our differing tolerance levels for spontaneity. I revel in the ability to make game-time decisions and to change things up midstream, while Ayla prefers a plan be committed in advance and adhered to. If we plan to have dinner with a set of friends, canceling the day-of because we scored last-minute Broadway tickets to *Hamilton* is a no-no. Impulsively buying each of my kids a toy at Target even though we just went for a shower curtain doesn't always light her up, especially if I did the same thing the day prior at Kohl's.

I crave novelty and unpredictability, while she sees a pile up of unnecessary purchases and other collateral damage (e.g., friends viewing us as unreliable). While this dynamic persists, we have come a long way in ten years, increasing our dialogue about decision-making and trying to strike a balance between sticking to the plan ("We are *only* getting a shower curtain at Target, no toys, agreed?") and welcoming a dose of unplanned fun (see: our loose approach to brilliant vacations).

CHILDREN AND PARENTS

As is true of life partners, our children have firsthand and often frustrating experiences of the ups and downs that we struggle with, and the way our own parenting journeys are affected.

On the upside, an adult with ADHD might be open to spontaneous play with their children. They may find that they're able to get into creative spaces and mindsets more easily.

On the downside, relationships with children can be strained when we're less able to meet the standard commitments of parenting, such as helping a child map out their homework, coming up with a plan for a class project, or carpooling on time. A sense of consistency, which can be very important for children, might be difficult for an adult with ADHD to provide if they have problems sticking to patterns and regular routines.

One of my clients who's struggling with ADHD is closing down a business and looking for a new opportunity while moving out of his home. His son is applying to college, and this requires the parent to submit documentation. Before he came to me, he had no way of managing the multiple tasks required of him, and he felt tremendous guilt. It was only through creating a task-management system, daily reminders, and other mindfulness-oriented tools that he was able to give his child the proper attention he needed at that crucial time in his life.

Meanwhile, as we've seen, the heredity of ADHD means that 40 to 50 percent of the children of an adult with ADHD will also have ADHD. The relationship between a parent and child who *both* have ADHD presents its own challenges.

I'm in the unique position of being raised by someone with ADHD, having it myself, and seeing it in at least two of my sons. These are all very different kinds of relationships, all affected in their own ways depending on the presenting symptoms and severity. There can be emotional dysregulation where they get heated quickly with each other. It can be hard to take a breath and slow down to work or talk through the frustrations that arise.

As a child, I was often frustrated with my mother's ADHD behavior. Why couldn't she remember the groceries we asked her to pick up that day? Why did she impulsively blurt out remarks that put other people off or embarrassed me or my siblings?

Now, as a parent with ADHD of children who likely have it as well, I'm seeing my mother's struggles in me and mine in my sons. My oldest son, now eight, struggles to sit still, he blurts things out, he's excitable—and he's completely brilliant. He's talked about existential concepts since three years old and ferociously reads two-hundred-page books. Yet I had to sit next to him during COVID-19 homeschooling just to keep him on track.

Parents with ADHD sometimes project their frustrations with themselves onto their children. Something the child does or experiences—for instance, struggling in school or with friends—can trigger the parent, who has probably experienced similar difficulties and only knows to respond in one way.

Again, there's a critical self-education component here that promotes and facilitates a deeper realization of what's going on—in yourself, your child, and your relationship with each other. This may not always make specific situations easier, but it does help to build better communication and empathy in the long run.

And of course, not everything about ADHD is tumultuous and frustrating. In fact, it even has some advantages. Let's look at a few before we move on.

Chapter 7

The Upside of ADHD

While it certainly comes with significant challenges, the ADHD brain also has several desirable strengths. Dr. Edward Hallowell, the mentor I worked with early in my career and the author of many influential books on ADHD (e.g. *Driven to Distraction* and *ADHD 2.0*), refers to the syndrome as "a gift one must learn to unwrap."

High rates of ADHD are found among entrepreneurs, CEOs, and artists, and for good reason. The upsides of ADHD include being innovative and thinking out-of-the-box, working well under pressure, being energetic, creative, and charismatic, and being savvy in interpersonal relationships, to name just a few.

As a clinical psychologist specializing in adult ADHD, I work with clients on developing a keen awareness of both their struggles *and* their strengths so they can achieve more of their potential. Though meeting the challenges of ADHD requires continual motivation and mindfulness and is rarely an easy process, the results can be life changing.

THE MIXED BAG THAT IS ADHD

Although it's undoubtedly challenging to move through this world with ADHD, the condition gets an unnecessarily bad rap. This is in part due to the medical model, which presumes every condition needs a cure or fix. It is stigmatized by being labeled a "disorder," and this perspective makes sense given ADHD's impact on children in the classroom and at home. As an adult with ADHD, I certainly have my own battle scars from those years.

But I've also experienced the myriad of benefits and bonuses that come packaged in the ADHD Cracker Jack box. Looking back at my own accomplishments, I can see where ADHD has contributed to each of them. This often rings true for others as well—not just my clients, but also well-known individuals with ADHD whose stellar accomplishments have made their names widely recognized.

These upsides include hyperfocus, creativity, spontaneity, exuberance, risk-taking, high performance under pressure, and intense passion. Of course, people without ADHD can exhibit any of these traits. And not every ADHD adult has each of these. However, there is a definite correlation between these traits and the syndrome's more positive aspects.

SPONTANEITY

The word "impulsive" tends to be associated with ADHD's more unfortunate outcomes. Being impulsive can get you into a lot of trouble. But there's an upside to being impulsive, captured by its near synonym, "spontaneous."

Spontaneity exists on a spectrum. Since ADHD adults are less inhibited, we filter out fewer ideas that pop up in our minds than our neurotypical counterparts. Our internal filtering system does much less editing before we express our ideas. Thinking of ten different ideas that I can't narrow down to one *can* be distracting, but the ability to come up with those ten different ideas when most people would limit themselves to one or two is also a strength. This makes us prone to being out-of-the-box thinkers. We're very good on our feet, especially in difficult or emergency situations.

People who are spontaneous are open to change, which means our lives and experiences are constantly changing. We're less anxiously self-protective, which again can lead to trouble, but also liberates us from restricting our range of possibilities.

The best vacations that Ayla and I take tend to be spontaneous, at least when it comes to details. I mentioned one such trip to California earlier in the book. Another that wound up coming together beautifully had been on our radar for nine months. We knew we wanted to take a summer vacation, but we didn't know when and we didn't know where. Then the summer came, and still without a plan, we continued to put it off until summer was nearly over.

Finally, we decided that August 20 would be our departure date—a Sunday morning. And the summer kept moving on until Friday, August 18 showed up. And we still had no plan. Massachusetts, Maine, Rhode Island, Canada…fly, drive, rent an RV…We discussed all of our options and couldn't come to anything that felt right. And Friday was upon us, with our observance of Sabbath nearing at seven in the evening, lasting through Saturday night at nine, with our scheduled departure of Sunday at seven in the morning. We were literally out of time!

At about six o'clock on Friday, like a flash of lighting illuminating the vast, dark sky with clarity, it all came together: we're taking a five-day road trip to Niagara Falls and Toronto, with fuzzy details in between. I booked a hotel for the first two days of the trip, checked that our passports were all valid, and shut my computer down for the Sabbath. The rest would unfold as we moved along.

Was it stressful? Of course—we had three kids under six and a largely unplanned road trip ahead of us. Did my wife and I have some tense moments? Yes. But was it another incredible last-minute adventure? Absolutely! We had a great time, probably because we've built up such a tolerance to last-minute, spontaneous things. For everything that *could* go wrong, these trips are a highlight of our family life, and we have my ADHD (and my wife's empathy, patience, and likely a touch of ADHD herself) to thank for it.

CREATIVITY

One of the ADHD's "deficiencies" involves the functioning of the prefrontal cortex, where planning and other executive functions, such as the ability to withhold a response and the awareness of the passage of time, take place. Yet the suppression of these apparently positive functions is not necessarily negative. In fact, it can lead to an immensely creative flow.

As we've seen, ADHD is caused in part to dopamine deficiencies. People with ADHD seek out the pleasures and rewards that accompany dopamine jolts and rushes. My own experience over the years is that I always get a dopamine rush when I launch a spontaneous, creative, out-of-the-box project or initiative.

There is a rush, a sense of stimulation, that comes from work that allows that creative potential to flow. It is no surprise, then, that artists of many types—musicians, actors, and the like—have faced and met the challenges of ADHD in ways that have benefited both themselves and those of us privileged enough to experience their artistry.

I'm going to name some names here and throughout this chapter but want to wave a yellow flag—a very un-ADHD thing to do—before proceeding. While some of the well-known names I'll be mentioning belong to people who've been diagnosed and are up-front about their ADHD, others have not. Let's say that some of what follows are informed guesses.

Comedians may be the most obvious examples of uninhibited artists whose work demands spontaneity of expression. What makes us laugh is often the unexpected and outrageous. Without a filter holding back those creative impulses, we get to see their spontaneity on full display.

Musicians are often extremely well-trained artists whose spontaneity and ability to bend and break the rules are what ultimately sets them apart. They're able to hyperfocus on their instrument. When that capacity for hyperfocus is directed toward their craft, and it's a craft that they love, they can create amazing works of art.

ENERGY, PASSION, AND HYPERFOCUS

Certainly, adults with ADHD can be easily distracted, but when something stimulates them—gives them the dopamine jolt they seek—they often dedicate an inordinate amount of time and attention to it. Within the ADHD sphere, "passion" is the best way of describing the experience people have when they get locked onto something they find highly stimulating, and it creates a tremendous amount of energy that can spur them to success.

Some top athletes, such as Michael Jordan, have been both challenged and strengthened by ADHD. Michael Phelps, who's still the greatest Olympic swimming champion, is another example of someone who was able to work long, dedicated hours because he was passionate about what he was doing. These athletes' high energy levels provide them, among other benefits, with much-needed mental stimulation.

High energy levels are common among my clients. The downside of this symptom is restlessness and difficulty sitting still. Because of this intensity, people with ADHD are often misdiagnosed as manic or bipolar. But those with ADHD who can channel their energy often produce innovative and groundbreaking products and ideas.

This manifests in me when I'm providing therapy, teaching, or presenting to large corporate audiences. I've certainly been challenged by my ADHD, but it's also helped me tremendously in my chosen work. The energy I'm able to spontaneously summon, even at an early hour of the morning, keeps students stimulated and awake. I've been told that I'm able to stand in front of a room of five hundred students and make it feel like an intimate space with only fifteen people present.

RISK-TAKING AND ENTREPRENEURSHIP

Gino Wickman, the bestselling author and creator of the Entrepreneurial Operating System (EOS) maintains that many if not most entrepreneurs are adults with greater or lesser levels of ADHD. This is a remarkable, even stunning, observation, given the importance of entrepreneurship in our economy.

Some of the best-known tech and other entrepreneurs have been diagnosed with or likely "suffer" from ADHD. These include Bill Gates, Richard Branson, and speculation around Elon Musk and the late Steve Jobs. Somewhat less known but still prominent entrepreneurs, such as David Neeleman of JetBlue and Ingvar Kamprad of Ikea, make the list as well.

Entrepreneurs, by definition, are risk-takers. People with ADHD, due to their proclivity to stimulation, are not averse to putting themselves in risky scenarios where there's no guarantee of success or a high possibility of failure. They can emotionally handle living on the edge.

There are introverted ADHD adults as well, but the extroverts are especially good at this. One of my clients is a highly successful real estate broker who is absolutely tenacious on the phone. He'll keep pushing himself and call a prospect at all hours of the day or night. He'll risk rejection, sounding ridiculous, and being told, "You're crazy," because his internal critic is louder than anything externally driven. The lack of inhibition and filtering once again plays a role here. Rejection, embarrassment, and failure just make them push themselves harder, and that's the kingmaker in the entrepreneurial world.

That isn't to say we won't struggle. I think of my client Olivia, who was passionate about men's fashion. She tried to start a line of men's ties and came up with any number of interesting, creative, and innovative ideas. Like many adults with ADHD, Olivia was able to generate thirty ideas and have samples ready for her big pitch, where others would be able to come up with a handful at a time.

Unfortunately, Olivia was subject to the downsides as well as the upsides of ADHD. She might get an order from a prestigious client such as Bloomingdale's, but she couldn't fill it. She got behind, her bookkeeping was a mess, and she couldn't hire anyone to do this work for her because she wasn't able to manage them.

The results were heartbreaking. Like chasing fireflies, Olivia would go in one promising direction, fail, and then come up with several promising ideas for other directions she might go in. She was taking the risks entrepreneurs are encouraged to take, but being a stand-alone businesswoman was not ideal for her particular manifestations of ADHD.

We ultimately worked toward helping Olivia wind down her business and shift toward working within a small company where she had externally established accountability and deadlines, as well as the support of a team to allow her to focus on her strengths of creativity and product design, leaving the sales, production, and back-office business management to others in the company. By reframing her relationship to both her strengths and weaknesses, along with constant tool refinement, Olivia was able to increase her probabilities of success on both a micro and macro level.

People with ADHD are great at initiating projects and tasks. But success involves more than this. There are hundreds and thousands of tasks on the road to success—those who succeed learn how to manage their tasks, whatever that might take. For example, they become adept at corralling other people who are strong in areas where they are weak. They become great at finding the right business partners, assistants, business coach, spouse, or all of the above. Done right, delegating and outsourcing can help you to unlock your strengths by clearing the path of what clogs the pipes of your dopamine-powered hyperfocus and flow.

Reaching and holding onto success as an adult with ADHD requires daily effort, with ongoing internal and external dialogue to reduce judgment, guilt, and shame for the moments we break stride from our achievement path. Engaging in tools and strategies such as task-management systems, accountability partners, and do-it-when-I-can meditation practices can all lead to improved probabilities of success, and that is the name of the game.

ADHD MEDICATION AND CREATIVITY: PROS AND CONS

We'll be dealing in-depth with ADHD medication somewhat later (see Chapter 19). But I should say here that I'm convinced medication can be an essential part of the ADHD treatment toolbox—*even though* there are some concerns about medication dampening the upsides of ADHD that we love about ourselves.

The bottom line is, when the cons of ADHD start to outweigh the pros, I've got to remember to apply my time-management, task-management, and mindfulness meditation tools. And depending on the day, I may need to take my ADHD medication to help me figure out where the waves have carried me and how I can get back to that sandcastle I had started with.

There's a big debate about this topic, but I will note that many adults that I work with who have ADHD report that they're less creative when they're on medication. They become more focused and able to complete what needs to be done, but they may end up unable to access as much of their creative palette as they're used to. They'll paint with two or three colors rather than twelve. Some of these clients are content that their medication helps provide a narrowed viewing scope with more regulated emotions and reduced impulsive tendencies, even if less "creative juice" comes to the surface as a result. It is not uncommon for such individuals to have a schedule that incorporates a few days off their medication every week or month that allows them to engage their creative minds in "default" mode (under the guidance of their prescribing doctor, of course). Others don't have the luxury of going off of medication due to the resulting executive and emotional dysfunction and thus will work with me to tap into creativity in other ways, such as meditation or brainstorming exercises.

Medication can take you out of the fog, giving you a crisp clarity that permits you to focus. It also puts a dam or levee down so that there isn't as much distracting stimulation flowing in—but by the same token, some claim there isn't as much exuberance and energy flowing out either.

On days when I teach at the university and am on my medication, my students know it. At home, my wife knows it. My affect becomes more limited, and my range of emotions narrows.

I don't always like that. I want to have that creative burst and flow. This presents a challenge to me and many other people with ADHD. Medication can make you feel like you're cut off from a good portion of your creativity, even though it also gives you the focus to be able to follow through. It's ultimately a matter of balance, relative to the severity of your symptoms alongside what's going to be happening in a given day.

I may wake up in the morning on a day where I have a lot going on. I look at my to-do list and get overwhelmed. I have things to do that I've been avoiding, and this is anxiety-producing. This is especially troublesome on days without a lot of structure in place, with few preset meetings and commitments, rather open-ended time that can easily be gobbled up by my expert avoidance and impulsive skillset.

Some days I make a conscious decision to take my medication because I know if I do, I'll get more done. Other days, there are other priorities that make it appropriate not to take medication. On some days it's a *got-to-have*, and on others it's a *cannot-have*. A good part of psychoeducation, and a big benefit of cultivating mindfulness, is being able to better determine which days are which—an increasingly difficult task in this era of constant distraction.

Chapter 8

Rewiring the Brain: Technology, Attention, and Memory

There is one final piece to the ADHD puzzle that we need to understand before we can begin to organize our chaos, and that is how pervasive technology has become in our lives and environment.

Many believe we have become "addicted" to technology, especially smartphones and social media. While "addiction" is a strong and sometimes overused term that may not be entirely accurate here, the concern does point to the extent of the issue's impact.

I refer to this impact as Techno-ADD, the cousin to clinical ADHD.[19] Techno-ADD affects far more people than clinical ADHD, and its symptoms and treatment are in many ways similar. Adults with ADHD may be affected with Techno-ADD as well, which can intensify the challenges they face.

While Techno-ADD and clinical ADHD are not the same, their overlap in the lives of those with adult ADHD demands attention and explanation, and this will be the focus of the next two chapters.

EXPONENTIAL CHANGE

Our technological revolution is above all a communications evolution. Yuval Noah Harari's bestseller *Sapiens: A Brief History of Humankind* does a spectacular job of detailing the importance of communications in human history.

For most of our history, communications were exclusively oral— sitting around fires, telling stories, and passing them along. The first great change in communication came with the invention of writing, and although it is rarely thought of as such, writing was itself a technology. It's worth noting that each time a new technology arises, there are complaints that, whatever the virtue of this technology might be, it's probably had the negative effect of reducing our memory capacity. This is true from as long ago as the time of the ancient Greeks.

The next great impact on communications—and what we more often think of as technology—came with the printing press. Over the last couple centuries, the pace of innovation has picked up, triggered by the invention of the telegraph and telephone. The pace of technological change then increased exponentially with the popular use of the internet in the mid-1990s. Cellphones were mass-marketed soon afterward.

It's difficult to grasp now, but the iPhone—the first smartphone combining communications and computing power—was only introduced in 2007. The advent of 3G in 2008, followed by networks with ever-increasing connectivity and speed, further accelerated the process. In just over a decade, mobile computing made Facebook, Instagram, WhatsApp, TikTok, and other social media platforms essential to most people's lives.

We had many years to adapt and acclimate to previous technological innovations. We no longer have that luxury. This exponential rate of change means that we have had far less time to adjust. Our brains are under constant strain while adapting to living, breathing, and functioning now that we are tethered to this new technology.

PHYSIOLOGY AND RESEARCH

The speed at which we have changed is unlike anything we have ever seen in the history of mankind, and this shift has occurred across the globe. I think that we're already seeing an impact on biology and brain structure, such as how our frontal lobes process information and our experiences.

Is technology in fact rewiring the brain? It's hard to know, although it's possible—particularly in infants and children. One thing that's certain is that our behavior is changing. People who would never be diagnosed with clinical ADHD are clearly developing the ADHD-like syndromes of Techno-ADD.

It takes the academic and scientific community several years to create systems for observing such new behavior, researching, analyzing, and assessing its impact. Yet technology today is evolving so fast that research can barely keep up. By the time we begin to understand the impact of Facebook, Instagram comes out, which is a whole different beast, and then TikTok came fast on its heels.

Instagram and TikTok will then be replaced or supplemented by—what? The "metaverse" with its virtual reality (VR) and augmented reality (AR) devices? Chips implanted onto our retina a la *Black Mirror*?[20] It's become difficult even to reflect upon, much less predict, the implications of our dependence on technology.

For example, in a 2018 Nielsen study, the average US adult was found to devote eleven hours per day to screen time.[21] If we're sleeping seven or eight hours a day, that doesn't leave a lot of nonscreen time. The COVID-19 quarantines and society shifts will no doubt leave a massive imprint on society, as what I believe to be the greatest psychological experiment of all time. Everyone from children to adults were plugged into screens from morning to night for work, school, and socialization. The long-term implications of this time, on top of the impacts of the pandemic itself, remain to be seen.

In the meantime, social media activity has already been on the rise for some time, with a 3 percent annualized growth rate. Worldwide social media usage as of January 2023 is at 4.76 billion people, equating to 59.4 percent of the total global population, with four new users joining social media *every single second*. According to Datareportal.com, the typical consumer spends an average of two and a half hours engaged in some form of social media each day. Assuming people sleep between seven and eight hours per day, this suggests that people spend roughly 15 percent of their waking lives using social media.[22]

Whether today's technology is actually changing the physiology of our brain and nervous system—and there is some indication it may be—its influence on how we receive and process the information in our environment is undoubtedly immense.

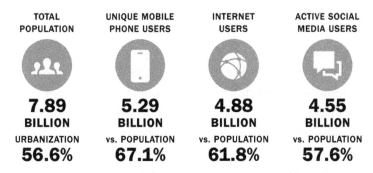

OCTOBER 2021. DIGITAL AROUND THE WORLD

TOTAL POPULATION	UNIQUE MOBILE PHONE USERS	INTERNET USERS	ACTIVE SOCIAL MEDIA USERS
7.89 BILLION	**5.29** BILLION	**4.88** BILLION	**4.55** BILLION
URBANIZATION 56.6%	vs. POPULATION 67.1%	vs. POPULATION 61.8%	vs. POPULATION 57.6%

Source: *www.smartinsights.com/social-media-marketing/social-media-strategy/new-global-social-media-research/*

Source: Chaffey, D. (2023, January 30). *Global social media statistics research summary 2023*. Smart Insights. https://www.smartinsights.com/social-media-marketing/social-media-strategy/new-global-social-media-research/

ADDICTION AND DEPENDENCE

Research suggests that there may be 210 million people across the globe who are addicted to the web and social media, representing 6 percent of social media users.[23]

Let's talk about these 210 million supposed social media addicts. Such addiction would be defined as a need to be on social media to the point where, when one goes off of it, they experience a strong pull and yearning to get back on. They experience high spikes of anxiety, and their social media use interferes with their functioning at home, in the workplace, or at school.

There's a lot of debate in the academic and medical community about using the word "addiction" in this context. I personally shy away from using the language of addiction. I prefer to use the terms "overdependence," "overreliance," and "tethering." Many people *are* tethered to and overdependent on their phones—but if a large number of people are engaging in a behavior that society seemingly accepts, are we sure we want to label it an addiction? What it really comes down to is the question we've already answered: does it affect functioning?

I think about this as like being in an unhealthy relationship. A relationship is unhealthy when you can't step away from it to the extent that your ability to function is affected. Like alcohol, in which one drink might be OK but being unable to stop can become debilitating, perhaps technology isn't an addiction outright, but rather holds the potential for addiction.

Regardless of the "everyone is doing it" factor, the skyrocketing rate of sleep problems and insomnia alone point to unhealthy behavior. This can be correlated with the use of cell phones at night. Seventy-three percent of people reported sleeping with their cell phones right next to or in their beds.[24] The phone is the last thing they look at before they go to bed and the first thing they check when they wake up in the morning. If this were any other substance or item, we would be very concerned.

THE FOUR DS

How serious is this overdependence on technology? For any mental disability or disorder, you would measure it against the so-called Four Ds: distress, dysfunction, dangerousness, and deviance. Let's look at each factor in turn.

Distress: It's true that many people love their smartphones and find using them very enjoyable. But if you inquire more closely, they also describe smartphone use as stressful. It's stressful to be on the phone so much, exposed to so many sources of information and able to see into so many people's lives. You feel like you *have* to constantly check your phone for messages and to see how many of your "friends" are going to "like" your most recent post. At some point, it has shifted from entertainment to necessary evil.

Dysfunction: My students often say they can't complete their studies because they're on the phone so much. When students use their laptops in their classroom, they're not focusing on what they're supposed to be learning.

Research shows that laptop use in the classroom is correlated with a full- or half-letter reduction in grade.[25] Someone who doesn't use a laptop in class might have gotten an A-. Using a laptop gives them a B+. Technology-induced workplace distractibility is no less a problem. While engaged in a Zoom meeting for work or school, how often are you checking your phone, engaging in multiple WhatsApp chats, checking the latest sports scores, stock ticker, or Instagram influencer's story? Doing so most certainly impedes your capacity for fully focused engagement with the primary meeting at hand. When functionality is clearly being affected, we're talking about dysfunction as well as distress.

Dangerousness: Simply look at the rates of texting while driving and the accidents that happen because people are using their cell phones or checking social media behind the wheel to get your answer here.

Ninety percent of drivers admit to using smartphones while driving. Fifty percent of those say they're checking social media. The Centers for Disease Control and Prevention says that nine people are killed and more than a thousand are injured as a result of smartphone use while driving—every day.

According to the National Highway Traffic Safety Administration, teens are the largest age group that drives while distracted by cell phone use.[26] I frequently see adolescents texting while riding bicycles and electric scooters. You can't tell me they're focusing on what's in front of them.

Lastly: is this deviant? Is it statistically out of the norm? It must be admitted that, right now, it's not. It is or is becoming the norm. This is why it's hard for society to accept that Techno-ADD is a problem that requires response.

I've been lecturing about the difficulties associated with technology use since the early 2000s, and at the time I was hard pressed to find anybody discussing the subject. The only thing people wanted to talk about was the positives of cell phones and other emerging technology. They didn't want to hear anything negative.

In more recent years, a critical trend is picking up. People are talking about the problems and the dangers of high tech. Even technology and media companies are doing so, pushing out native apps to monitor screen time, tech health, and other measures to increase mindful use of technology. There's greater recognition of the downsides and the beginnings of a dialogue.

Will our attitudes shift as we become more aware of the dangers of overdependence on technology? I believe the shift is already starting to happen. Multiple consumer groups have sprouted up to speak to this issue, and Netflix and other streaming services have featured documentaries that raise the alarms (e.g. *The Social Dilemma, Life 2.0, Like*). The question is whether we'll be able to adapt our behavior in response.

BEHAVIORAL ISSUES AND QUALITY OF LIFE

Despite the lag in research, there are numerous studies already giving evidence that cell phone use is having a detrimental effect on the quality of our lives. I've mentioned one already: the effect on sleep. Insomnia indicates that people have unhealthy relationships with their smartphones.

Though they're a powerful communications medium, digital interactions are also taking the place of interpersonal and in-person social interactions, even or perhaps especially in the family. Children are commonly reporting that their parents aren't paying as much attention to them because they are on their phones. The term "continuous partial attention" has been coined to describe this phenomenon. Adults also report that their kids aren't communicating and interacting with either their parents or their peers because of heavy phone dependence.

Beginning to sound familiar yet? Any ADHDisms coming to mind?

There are also anecdotal reports of children having tantrums when their parents force them to stop using technology even for short periods. When you pry a phone away from a six-year-old, they often go crazy. This is a very different experience than what watching television was because the relationship is bidirectional or mutual.

As kids watch television, they are for the most part passive. With mobile phones, tablets, and social media, on the other hand, there's a feedback loop involving the neurotransmitter dopamine, which people with clinical ADHD crave. When someone gets thirty likes on Instagram, they get a dopamine rush. Once that passes, there's a craving for more. That's why people go back to check their phones again and again.

The reinforcement loop is both positive and negative. If I check my phone and something desirable is waiting for me, I experience pleasure. If I look at my phone and there's nothing there, I experience a little bit of suffering or pain. To reduce that pain and anxiety, I'll keep checking until I find something positive waiting.

Being so tightly tethered to our devices yields a slightly to more pronounced gap between us and the present moment. We trade the deeper connection with our physical and natural environment, as well as to those present in it, for a highly dependent relationship with the digitally presented world.

ATTENTION SPAN AND MEMORY

There's a lot of talk about technology diminishing our attention spans. Some claim the length of that span has shifted from twelve to nine seconds, which is often asserted to be the attention span of a goldfish.

This notion may have caught fire because it sounds believable. Certainly, many people feel their attention spans are shorter than they used to be. But it's doubtful that our physiology has been affected since our actual human cognitive capacity for attention is still the same. The originating, then viral, "goldfish" claim itself was misconstrued—but there is something worth noting underlying it. Technology has divided people's attention and weakened our memory.

I used to be able to remember my schedule, my friends' phone numbers, and many birthdays by heart. That is no longer the case. Neuroscientist Véronique Bohbot at McGill University has been studying this trend and presented her findings at the Society for Neuroscience's annual meeting in 2010.

Dr. Bohbot found that using smartphone features like the address book, calendar, and GPS reduces reliance on our hippocampus, the brain structure that controls memory. With the hippocampus, like any other body part, you have to "use it or lose it," and that part of the brain appears to be reducing in strength and size as we outsource our memories to digital devices. Perhaps our physiologies are indeed beginning to change.

The need for instant gratification—something typical of those with clinical ADHD—is increasing in the general population. We don't watch Netflix, we binge watch. We can't wait a week to watch the next episode. We have to watch it and the following six episodes immediately.

Netflix has changed its refresh time from thirty seconds or so down to fifteen, and by the time you read this chapter, it may be down to five seconds. This creates a dopamine rush that increases our dependence. Netflix and the other streaming services are capitalizing on our increasingly Techno-ADD minds.

Is the cause of this biological or behavioral? Again, it's too early to tell. Perhaps the same mechanisms are operating in clinical ADHD and Techno-ADD. We just don't know yet. What we do know is that the distractions of Techno-ADD negatively impact functioning in relationships and at work.

We've also looked at the overlap among clinical ADHD, anxiety, and dependence. In fact, there's an interrelationship between dependence of any kind and anxiety and depression: you're anxious for the next hit and depressed when you're deprived.

Although our focus is on adult ADHD, we have to acknowledge that technology and its effects are more ubiquitous for the younger generation—those who are called digital natives. Their brains don't know of any alternatives to digital technology. Those who are older know what it's like to not be tethered. Our brains recollect what it's like to live without that constant magnetic pull.

The implications of this are still unknown. Objectively speaking, there may not be that much difference between the effects of Techno-ADD on digital natives and digital immigrants.[27] The net result is that neither digital natives nor digital immigrants are as present in their interpersonal conversations as they could be. Both have higher risks of automobile accidents and suffering from sleep issues.

These problems exist across the spectrum, but I do think there is a difference in terms of the level of insight about it: digital natives don't know there are different ways to live and relate. That makes education only half the battle—we have to teach them a new way of seeing the world.

Chapter 9

———

Responding to Techno-ADD

Technology, as we've seen, can easily become a vortex of distraction. Social media and web browsing soon become overwhelming: "I end up with so many tabs open that I lose sight of what I originally sat down to work on."

As a psychologist, I sometimes look at web browsing as the modern-day version of Freudian free association: letting the mind wander and loosely jumping from one idea to the next, with barely a faint connection between any two links in the chain.

Fortunately, there are some very practical steps you can take to reassert control. First, let's look a little more at the similarities between Techno-ADD and clinical ADHD and how today's technology can intensify ADHD symptoms. Then we can move on to solutions.

THE RIPPLE EFFECT

The heavy use of technology—being tethered to devices—has yielded ripple effects on our brains' executive-function systems, and particularly the ability to maintain sustained or prolonged attention on a single or repetitive activities. A core symptom of ADHD is distraction, being pulled from one task to another. People with ADHD can't endure long periods of focus on tasks they don't find stimulating.

Smartphones are seemingly made to be as distracting as possible. Perhaps you check your phone once an hour, or five or six times an hour. Perhaps every ten minutes. To be clear, the app developers, programmers, and content creators actually want you to focus, but on *their* content—thereby distracting you from everything else, even if for only ten to thirty seconds at a clip. Statistics show that many people get into zones where they're checking their phones every four minutes.[28]

How can you sustain your focus on the task at hand when your hand is constantly diving into your pocket or pocketbook to check for that latest tweet, post, gram, or TikTok video? That's very much a distracted, ADHD-type experience.

The ability to avoid distraction and maintain focus in the face of competing stimuli is called "selective attention." When trying to work on something, ADHD makes it difficult to ignore external stimuli pulling at your attention. In a meeting or lecture, people with ADHD are more likely to have their attention dart out the window to look at a passing airplane, or notice someone scratching their head, or become distracted when a delivery arrives.

The symptoms of Techno-ADD are very similar. It's very hard

for people, when they feel a buzz in their pocket or hear a beep from any one of their twenty to a hundred apps with notifications, not to check what's happening immediately. Or to jump back and forth between work-related browser tabs, a Reddit tab, or another personal browser tab. Even those without clinical ADHD are finding it much harder to delay this kind of gratification.

More and more of us are very dependent on and have poor relationships with our phones as well as poor awareness of our phone use. While trying to work, we see an email come in from a retail store we subscribe to. We click through, thinking this will only take half a minute. Then twenty minutes pass and we're deep into shopping mode, having jumped over onto Amazon, searching different categories, while reading through the digital *Farmer's Almanac's* predictions of weather for summer 2025 since we want to plan that anniversary vacation. Such symptoms of Techno-ADD have become pervasive. While this may not be clinical ADHD, which is a biological and developmentally based disorder, it looks and smells a whole lot like it.

Techno-ADD is often accompanied by fidgetiness—a tapping of hands or feet and squirming around, especially when on the phone. This is not exactly but very similar to what an ADHD person experiences. Much of this is due to attention being split between the phone and whatever else is happening, such as trying to have a conversation or a meal with someone.

Another similarity is decreased inhibition. People can no longer inhibit themselves from checking their phones. When waiting in line at the bank or on a New York subway platform, it's very difficult for people to stop themselves from checking and engaging with their mobile apps. They can't sit, be self-reflective, and just present with their own thoughts.

In earlier times, people used to read newspapers on subways and books or magazines on planes. Now the interaction is bidirectional rather than passive. Now people carry around devices that engage and pull at them everywhere they go.

Does everyone who gets into the "got to constantly check my smartphone" zone have clinical ADHD? Certainly not. But the symptoms of Techno-ADD are certainly very similar, and people with ADHD tend to use that technology to aggravate already existing tendencies.

DEAR TECHNOLOGY

Although the syndrome has gotten more noticeable and intense with the passing years, it has been building for some time now. I've been noticing this tendency for a while and did a few blog posts entitled "Dear Technology" for the online version of *Psychology Today* about the time that Steve Jobs passed away in 2011.

At Jobs's passing, I recalled that, in 1990, about eight years after the introduction of the Mac, he said, "What a computer is to me is the most remarkable tool that we have ever come up with. It's the equivalent of a bicycle for our minds."

Eleven years later, however, in a 2001 *Newsweek* article, Jobs was singing a different tune, saying, "I would trade all my technology for an afternoon with Socrates." Technology's ability to enhance our lives clearly comes with limitations.

Many have speculated that Jobs, the person as responsible as anyone for the invention of the smartphone, would have been unhappy and discouraged at people's current dependence on the device. It was meant to be a tool for us to use rather than one to use us.

Psychologist Dr. Sherry Turkle, a professor at MIT, is one of the most thoughtful students of and writers on this subject. In her book *Alone Together: Why We Expect More from Technology and Less from Each Other*, she asserts that our relationships with portable devices "may offer the illusion of companionship without the demands of friendship" (p. 1).[29]

Companionship without friendship doesn't sound like a particularly healthy relationship. As I've mentioned, our ties to technology have in many cases become dependent. Any healthy relationship requires creating and maintaining boundaries, and we need to make sure these boundaries are real and tangible, not just metaphorical. What we need is to make technology our partner rather than our adversary.

DIGITAL WELL-BEING

If you suffer from Techno-ADD—whether the dopamine rushes of techno-dependence add to the challenges of underlying clinical ADHD or not—you will benefit from many of the tools to come in the remainder of the book. To begin, there are steps that can be taken to increase what I call your digital well-being. None of these is complicated—in fact, they're all fairly simple—but they demand that you take action to draw boundaries and establish "technology-free zones" in your life. Let's go through a few of them.

Tech-free times. Designate times of your day or your week where you're willing to separate from your phone and other devices. It could be breakfast, lunch, or dinner. If this feels too difficult, start with shorter time periods, like when you're crossing the street. When you're about to cross the street, put your phone in your pocket or pocketbook and don't touch it. Take the ten seconds it takes you to cross the street to live without your phone. An elevator ride is another time-hop you can take without your phone in hand, just to create the awareness that separation is possible and in your control.

For me personally, I feel my family needs me more at dinnertime than I need my Twitter feed. So I silence my phone and put it out of sight and off my person—in a drawer, a designated shoebox, or even a paper bag. This physical barrier prevents me from impulsively checking my cell phone before realizing I'm even doing so. The only way I can get to my phone for a specific purpose is to physically remove that barrier.

Tech-free zones. Given today's rash of insomnia, it's critical to establish your bedroom as a tech-free zone. Especially when you're going to sleep at night, your phone should not be in your room at all.

People tell me all the time, "But I need it to help me wake up."

I tell them, "I know this sounds crazy, but I just heard the announcement of a great invention called an alarm clock. Buy it with some double-A batteries, put it next to your bed, and let that wake you up. Then put your phone in another room to charge overnight so it's not pulling you."

Tech-free zones don't need to be limited to the bedroom or even the home. If you're going to a meeting, put your phone in a drawer in your desk beforehand. You'd be surprised to learn that many companies in the tech sector promote phone-free meetings, realizing the negative effects the device has on focus and attention. (This irony is not lost on me—I wonder if they've caught on yet.)

Delete apps. Another important way to create balance and digital well-being is to minimize the number of apps on your phone. How many are there now? They're so easy to download that they proliferate like rabbits. Take a look right now and decide which five apps you don't need. Now delete them. In fact, maybe the number of apps you could delete would be twenty rather than five.

How many apps are on your home screen? Which are core apps that you use for real productivity and communications? Which don't you need and are just distractions? Limit your home screen to the select few you absolutely need from the former category.

Game apps in particular are distractions that do you no favors. Game developers design games to make them addictive. They're fighting against you. Do you have the courage to get rid of them? Many of my clients who have done this have said, "That changed my life! I've gotten hour after hour of my day back."

Not that long ago, smartphones meant text messages and the occasional missed call. Now, people have 102 apps on their phone, each primed to deliver a carefully titrated and reinforcing dopamine boost. Believe me, you'll live better without them.

Email management. Depending on who you are, email and social media are the number one distractors. For me, email comes out on top in the distraction sweepstakes. Email is nonstop and overwhelming, so developing systems to manage your email is crucial.

One approach is to designate times of the day for email checking. Perhaps this is from 10:00 to 11:00 a.m. You may choose to check email twice a day instead, but you'll soon realize that less is more. Incidentally, there is a Gmail setting that turns off automatic email notifications so that you aren't bothered whenever an email arrives, which will help you focus on what you really have to do. I have several clients who run their own companies or divisions who created top-down policies that no internal emails should be exchanged between specific hours, such as 8:00 p.m. to 8 a.m. As you can imagine, it has become quite a popular "perk" among employees.

More broadly, one approach that works well is to partition usage of specific technology into different sections of the day. There could be one part of the day, as just mentioned, for email and another for social media and networking. Most of the day should be focused on work or study.

Tracking. One good way to start limiting your technology use is to track it. Use technology to limit technology. Get a good spreadsheet or app that enables you to keep track of how much time you spend online in a sitting. As you web surf, keep track of every site you visit. Then, to ensure you don't get lost down a rabbit hole, set an alarm—yes, perhaps on your phone—for twenty-five minutes. When the alarm sounds, it's time to stop web surfing! As mentioned above, many phones now have native systems in place for just such monitoring.

Children and parents. I have young children and know that the struggle with technology is very real for parents. It's critical to set limits as early as possible. The more clearly limits are set, the fewer tantrums there will be when technology needs to be temporarily taken away. My wife and I have adopted a strong stance on technology. After all, this is about our kids' quality of life. Smartphones should not be used to pacify children. Although we own tablets for our kids, we initially used them only on rare occasions, such as when we're flying or on long car rides. Over time and as the kids get older, we adjust the limitations, whereby now we allow tablets for a limited time on Sundays.

The above is not meant to be an exclusive list but to prompt you to develop your own ways to limit your dependence on and create a better relationship with technology.

MINDFUL AWARENESS

The most important cause of Techno-ADD is simply being unaware or unconscious of the extent of smartphone and other technology use. Recently, awareness of the problem has increased, as more people are finally beginning to see the negative impact of their overuse of technology. Even executives at tech giants such as Google and Facebook are stepping away from their desks to acknowledge the problem in public.

We have gotten to the point where we don't feel we exist unless we have a digital or social media footprint. That's certainly the reality for the younger generations of digital natives.

All the therapeutic techniques we'll explore in the coming chapters will help you meet the challenges of both clinical ADHD and Techno-ADD. As I've mentioned, underlying them all is the practice of mindful awareness.

Mindful awareness and mindfulness meditation are becoming a far more prominent part of the conversation throughout society. Mindfulness just means focusing on the experience of what is going on in your mind without being distracted or tethered by whatever else is going on.

All the mindfulness-based and behavioral treatments that can be applied to ADHD are also valuable in dealing with Techno-ADD. These include meditation techniques, behavioral modification, the ability to observe and track behavior to determine what needs to be changed, limit-setting, and alternative rewards systems. Developing improved relationships though awareness training, including an improved relationship with your own mind and thoughts, has direct application to both clinical ADHD and Techno-ADD.

And, having gone through some extensive psychoeducation around both adult ADHD and Techno-ADD, it's time to move on to interventions to meet and overcome the challenges of both syndromes.

PART III

Life Hacks: Behavior Change

Chapter 10

—

Get Organized

Many of us struggle to hit the "go" button in the morning and launch into the workday, which means we often waste our mornings Instagram scrolling, online shopping, or news binging. Away from the screen, we spend too much time talking politics, catching up with colleagues, or talking about last night's game.

Once we do buckle down and get to work, other challenges arise. Most people's schedules require them to shift from one task to another at different times of the day. This can be difficult for adults with ADHD. Once we get into a dopamine-infused, hyperfocused groove, it's difficult to switch gears.

Without a solid, ADHD-friendly system, you'll end up anxious, inefficient, and barely effective, and you will often avoid your most important tasks altogether. If your approach to managing your life consists of a single to-do list put together without any organizational forethought, the waves of ADHD will still come—and they'll take you *and* your mess of organizational tools out to sea.

When working with clients, after educating them about what ADHD is—and what it isn't—I often turn to skill building before anything else. The focus at this stage is on helping them learn how to use a set of practical organizational skills and planning tools to overcome such ADHD tendencies as procrastination, perfectionism, and not getting things done. Once we get an upper hand on some of the executive-functioning issues that plague my clients, we also tend to see relief from the byproducts and frustration that led them to my office in the first place.

Take Rose, for example. She's a mother of four who has an at-home business creating custom stationery, as part of a dual-income household. She reached out to me when managing the house, her work, and the kids' school schedule became unmanageable during the initial peak of COVID homeschooling. Her relationship was suffering, her sleep was completely interrupted, and at times she felt like she could barely come up for air.

Our plan of attack included weekly meetings on Sunday nights with her husband so they could go over what had to happen during the upcoming week at home so the tasks could be mapped out and more evenly distributed. We created meditation and exercise plans for her to try out. And most importantly, we helped her become significantly more mindful of her own emotional state so that she could take more time for herself. Did everything land and last with perfection? Certainly not, as it rarely does. But we succeeded in elevating her overall awareness, provided paradigms for viable ADHD tools, and gave her a greater handle on increasing her probabilities of success.

These kinds of organizational life hacks are also known as "behavioral interventions." Simply put, we're giving adults with ADHD ways to adjust their behaviors, elevate their self-awareness, and increase the likelihood of meeting the challenges that come with their ADHD. You may find, as many of my clients do, that this one of the most practical and impactful sections of this book and of your approach to treating ADHD.

While there are many life hacks and behavioral interventions to apply for all presentations of ADHD, let's set the stage by first explaining the dichotomy of ADHD's default *now vs not now* sorting mechanism.

NOW VS NOT NOW

When an ADHD person is presented with a task, they tend to filter it into one of two categories: "now" and "not now." Time blindness makes it difficult to think specifically about the future or to plan what's to come and what needs to be done.

A few years ago, my family and I were traveling to Jamaica, and I knew eight months in advance that we would need passports to do so. But instead of eight months, I thought of it as "not now." I didn't put it into my organization system, and I didn't think twice about it. Suddenly, eight months turned into ten days, and the task *now* was very different than it had been at *not now*. Instead of a simple errand, I had to take off work, pay extra for an expedited process, deal with an unexpected snowstorm, and more.

Hitting the *not now* snooze button provides great relief from task anxiety in the short term, but often yields a spike of doomsday anxiety once time runs out, and *now* becomes the only remaining option with nothing but haphazard hyperfocus to see the task through. A key element to more effectively deal with the *now vs not now* dynamic is to establish an ADHD- friendly task-management system.

Few of my clients have an organizational system when I begin working with them. Many don't have any lists at all and simply depend on their memory to decide what particular tasks they need to get done and when. They're under the misconception that they will be able to recall important tasks at the right time, then shift from one task to another as appropriate.

This is a bear trap. Without an organizational system that you can actually use, most tasks tend to get put in the "not now" category and are pushed out of sight, often until it is too late, or nearly so.

As we've seen, the systems—including memory—of those with ADHD are relatively divergent. A good task-management system will help reduce dependence on working memory, and that is where external organizational tools come in.

QUALITIES OF ADHD-FRIENDLY ORGANIZATIONAL SYSTEMS

Among the top challenges adults with ADHD face is time and task management. Whether you're a student, lawyer, real estate broker, homemaker, teacher, or entrepreneur, you have a list of things that need to get done.

There might be a few half-used yellow pads laying around, Post-its stuck around the desk, that one shiny new app (or several), a few napkin scribbles, and everything in between. Or you might have no external lists at all, just that mental pen and scratchpad that seems efficient enough until you need to go "looking" for something. With so many planners, apps, and strategies that one can choose from—how do you narrow it down?

Three key components can make a decent organizational system especially helpful for someone with ADHD. Look for:

- A dashboard or bird's-eye view of your tasks organized by category
- A method for pulling down from bird's-eye view to today's targeted goals
- A way to pin today's tasks to specific times or blocks of time

Add a sprinkle of digital reminders, a pinch of external accountability, and a dash of self-compassion for when the system temporarily falls apart or drops out of sight, and you too can savor the taste of increased probabilities of success.

For those among you hell-bent on sticking with all or parts of your current method for task management, I encourage you to see if at the very least, some elements can be upgraded. For others who have never used a formal system or yearn for an alternative that works better than what you've tried, buckle up. This system is a game changer.

3-TIER TASK MANAGEMENT

The bedrock of my approach to task (and time) management is the *3-Tier System*, which starts off on a broad weeklong view of your tasks, objectives, to-do's etc., organized by category; then funnels from the week view down to daily tasks; finally bringing you to an hour-by-hour, or blocked-time handle of your day's intentions. By funneling down from a large-scale view to when I *think* I might get specific tasks done within a day, I can increase my probability of success over a given week and reduce the power of procrastination and perfectionism which when unfettered, can rule the day. You can find these templates on my site, DrSitt.com, if you'd like to download or print your own. You can also check out PlannerPads.com for a similarly oriented system, which can be purchased as a bound organizer.

Let's go one Tier at a time to see how to make the most of it.

PLANNING FOR THE WEEK OF: May 15 – May 21, 2022

TIER 1: WEEKLY LIST OF ACTIVITIES BY CATEGORIES

PRIVATE PRACTICE	BIZ FINANCIALS/ACCTNG	BARUCH COLLEGE	HOME/FAMILY	FINANCIALS/PERSONAL	FAMILY VACATION	MISC (SBH, OTHER)
sign up for CE Credits	QB billing (ongoing)	recruit new TA	Passport 4 Frieda & Ezra	f/u w Pearsons credit ln	finalize dates w/Ayla	Get mom ER ID band
Apply for NJ License	fix Bluehost for drsitt.com	1001 - consider new text	get new insurance quote	f/u on DeCaP	ask Jason's fam to join	check JetBlue 5k points
Ping lapsed Pts		1001 - set up assnmt cal	10 yr anny vacay	donation to SBH	Bonvoy choices?	resolve MDM donation Q
Fire up website dev again	Mirsky call re: Tax	3077 - launch class blog	call Emblem re: ADHD Rx	call Visa re: Refund	check out Hershey Park	return NYP Library books
f/u networking email		3077 - grade exam (120m)	shelves for ezras room	f/u re: living will/ POA	Montreal road trip option?	get car inspection
create title for NYU talk			Return VZ cable boxes BK	pay gardener	buy new suitcase	
			call electrician	meet with 401k advisor		
ADHD Refocussed Project	Thrive Project	AFN Project	send ADT info to insurance			
send to Ramsey	Productivity module text	present 3 wellbeing traings	chimney check			
f/u to pelcovitz	review comp apps	burnout/remote work opt	Costco run			
finalize ToDo List		EQ profile with Steve	replace broken TV			

TIER 2: DAILY THINGS TO DO

MONDAY	TUESDAY	WEDNESDAY	THURSDAY	FRIDAY	SATURDAY	SUNDAY
Go Through Mail Pile	title for NYU talk	3077 - grade exam (60m)	3077 - grade exam (60m)	QB billing	Off for Shabbat	research new TV
call re: hospital bill	pay gardener	f/u DeCap	Steve EQ profile mtg	Mirsky call re: Tax		work on NJ license
Thrive: work on module 1	pay Dennis C	prep for Steve EQ profile	call for 401k advisor mtg	buy suitcase		prep Ezras hockey bag
email Dr.P re: book endorse	3077 - launch blog	call for Chimney Check	call aunt Tunie	take car for inspection		Jonah math HW review
Monday plans	donation to SBH	Go to Costco	return VVZ cable boxes	send out TA job posting		take Natan to bday party
1001 - new text book?	Anne W Balance	Finalize Vacay Dates	finalize TA job description			Frieda haircut
send pt email check ins	call Mom	speak to Jason re: Vacay				call Hershey Hotels
sign up for 4 CE credits		draft TA job description				

TIER 3: HOURLY + APPOINTMENTS (See Next Tabs)

My 3-Tier Spreadsheet for mid-May 2022

TIER 1: WEEKLY

A key element to Tier 1 is the arrangement of tasks into categories, which immediately brings a greater degree of organization than the typical undifferentiated everything-and-all list that some may use. So in this first portion, I list out all the tasks I would *ideally* like to get done, or that I have on my radar, over the next week or two. In reality, I often include tasks that might be due a few weeks out as well, as I'd rather have them on the radar early than rely on my memory to add them down the line.

As you can see in the example of my 3-Tier spreadsheet, my categories are **Private Practice** (for general matters pertaining to my therapy practice), **Biz Finances/Accntg** (all matters pertaining to the finances of my business and my accountant notes), **Baruch College** (which covers my university-related responsibilities), **Home/Fam** (covering home responsibilities, errands, grocery shopping, my children, etc.), **Financials-Personal** (all personal financial matters, such as paying bills, credit cards, donations, medical bills, etc.), **Family Vacation** (for planning an upcoming trip), and **Misc** (covering anything that may not neatly fit into other categories). I included a few additional categories at the bottom of Tier 1 that pertain to some targeted projects I am working on: the **ADHD Refocused** book project, **Thrive Project** (an adult ADHD app that I am consulting on, which is now called Agave Health), and **AFN Project** (a corporate coaching/consulting client). The categories on the top of Tier 1 tend to stay mostly the same, but can certainly shift with time and circumstance, whereas the bottom projects are variable depending on what's coming in and out of focus.

What categories do *your* life's obligations and tasks fall into? Take a moment now to jot down what you believe to be your six to eight categories.

For some, coming up with categories happens in a flash. Others may struggle to do so, as they rarely think beyond the work/home dichotomy of tasks. In that case, don't overthink this—just make a raw task list first, and from there, see if you can glean categories from what you see in front of you. Honing down to the categories that make the most sense for your life can be a trial-and-error process that takes a few weeks to work through.

THE BRAIN DUMP

If you are having trouble getting started with the *3-Tier System*, here are preliminary steps that can help you begin the process:

1. Start by taking out a blank piece of paper or opening a Word document.
2. List everything that you need to get done over the next one to two weeks.
3. Once everything is on the table, begin to look for patterns to categorize them.
   a. i.e., finish presentation, submit invoice—create a "Work" category.
   b. i.e., buy pet food, pick up materials from hardware store—create a "Personal" category.
4. Once you have the categories, take them to your sheet and begin to place tasks under each one.

What to List in Tier 1

With your categories laid out, place them at the top section of Tier 1. Underneath each category, list out all the tasks you hope to get done, or scratch the surface of, over the next few weeks. Numbering the tasks in each respective category is optional but can help quantify what you need to take care of. In general, enumeration takes more of the disorganization and mystery out of an otherwise jumbled ADHD brain.

Clients often ask, "What type of tasks should be included in Tier 1?" I generally advise that tasks be broken down into subsets as often as possible. Rather than making "plan my wedding" a task, it's much better to list out what planning steps are needed for the week. These might include *Call the Florist, Visit Three Dress Shops*, and *Plan a Test Photo Shoot*. These are quantifiable, achievable steps that won't be overwhelming when you see them on the list. As an aside, with this particular example, you likely would create "Wedding" as a category itself, listing out the specific tasks for that multiweek period.

Putting down *Do Research for Lecture* makes the task vague, and the ADHD brain doesn't do well with vague. Such ambiguity is intimidating, to the extent that I might avoid doing the task altogether. *Read Three Articles*, on the other hand, is tangible. Then in Tier 2, I might map out my plan to read one article on Monday, two on Tuesday, and summarize them on Wednesday. Quantification makes it easier for my brain to wrap itself around and commit to doing a task.

On occasion, I recommend that large tasks, such as planning a wedding, working on a quarterly report, or writing a term paper, get a bit of an expansion. List all the substeps for the larger project in a separate section of your planner, spreadsheet, or app. Then, as you move from week to week, you can pull in the relevant tasks for a particular week from that larger project list.

When to Work on Tier 1

I advise clients to get Tier 1 written out over the weekend, perhaps on Sunday night, and at the very latest by Monday morning. The idea is to have it ready *before* you jump into the flow of your work/school week. You want to be in a calm and clear headspace while laying out Tier 1, not already in the rocky rapids. As the week progresses, you will be checking off, adjusting, and editing Tier 1. And come the next weekend, you are to open up a fresh new page, and start Tier 1 all over again. The notion is that by doing a refresh each week, you will have direct feedback as to what tasks are being avoided like the plague, need reconfiguring, and potentially cut out as unrealistic expectations at the present time.

As for written vs digital, I prefer a hybrid model, whereby I type up my Tier 1 into the 3-Tier planning spreadsheet (again, located at DrSitt.com), then print it out, and use a pen to make my edits for the rest of the week, until I rehash it over the next weekend. Having a printed copy keeps my system tangible and in eyeshot at all times, rather than having it lost among various digital tabs, apps, and a cascade of screen-dependent resources.

Engaging my system in a tactile way—with a pen and paper, with checkmarks, strikeouts, and scribbles—helps to deepen my relationship with the system. In fact, research comparing depth of processing and retention of information entered through keystrokes versus handwriting (e.g., with college students in a classroom) suggests that one retains information better through handwriting (assuming it's legible!).[30] If I keep it entirely digital, whether through apps or a spreadsheet, I miss out on an integral layer of depth of neural processing.

TIER 2: DAILY

From our macro level Tier 1 view, we can funnel the week down to a daily plan of action on Tier 2. Before the start of each respective day (e.g., the night before or early the day of), look at all you have listed in Tier 1 to remember what you'd wanted to do for the week. Then, in that day's Tier 2 column (e.g., Monday, Tuesday, etc.), list out those tasks or subtasks that you think you *might* be able to knock out on that day.

I also suggest that at the very beginning of your week, just after completing your Tier 1 dump, see which Tier 1 tasks can be earmarked to specific days of the week ahead and enter those on the respective days in Tier 2, even if just one or two per day. This further "loosens the cap" of anxiety about how you'll plan the upcoming week.

Most items on Tier 2 daily lists will be extrapolated from what is written in Tier 1 under the "Categorical" view. Tasks such as *Pay Amex Bill*, *Return Clothes to GAP*, and *Finalize Client Presentation*, are not multilayered tasks. For tasks listed in Tier 1 that ARE multilayered or complex, it is here in Tier 2 that we try to sparse out a few small, easy-to-achieve substeps of such larger tasks/goals. So if I have *Prepare Taxes* under my "Personal Finances" T1 category, on Thursday's T2 I might list the specific tasks of *Find Donation Receipts* and *Download W-2*, and on Friday's T2 I might list, *Get Mortgage Yr-End Stmt*. Note the shorthand too. It helps to be informal, save space, and just get the job done.

As an aside, for certain very large goals or projects, you might wish to create a separate reference document where you thoroughly break down and outline the project/goal into substeps and tasks, then feed a few tasks at a time into Tier 1, adding more as you knock off the previous ones. A third type of task that you might jot down on T2 is something that comes up out of the blue, that isn't even on T1, but must get done that day, such as *Buy Milk, Call Mom Back*, or *Get Gas*.

Funneling from a broad Tier 1 view to a limited scope Tier 2 daily view helps cut down the likelihood of being overwhelmed by too many choices in the moment when you're ready to begin working.

If I see *Get a Job* on my general to-do list, I might have a panic attack. *What does that mean? Where do I begin? I can't deal with this now!* I'll just snooze this item and put it in the "not now" category until I face a cliff that forces me to finally hyperfocus on the task.

The challenge is not necessarily with the task, rather in how I frame the objective. *Get a Job* is too nebulous. It simply isn't in my power to snap my fingers and get a job. With my 3-Tier System, I would list "Job Hunt" as one of my categories and list out several in-my-control, small, achievable steps that I'd try to execute in the next few weeks. Then, I would work these tasks into my Tier 2 level, adding a few steps across various days of the week. I would limit each daily list to a few items, such as:

- Send out ten resumes.
- Call three employment agencies.
- Take interview suit to drycleaners.

Getting such tasks done *is* in my control, and I'm much more likely to use that list.

The framing of our expectations for success is a key element to Tier 2, and to task management overall. With daily lists, I have found it extremely helpful to shift expectations of success away from 100 percent. For me, **80 percent is the new 100.**

Let's say my daily list contains twelve items. If I expect to get all twelve done, I'll nearly always be disappointed. But if 80 is the new 100, I can get seven or eight of the twelve done and still feel great.

Perfection is overrated!

When we practice 80 as the new 100 in our organizational systems, by the time we get to mindfulness we'll realize that 60 percent is the new 80 percent and is just as good. The more we can expand the bull's-eye to redefine what a "win" is, we can hit it more often and find satisfaction in our lives more regularly.

TIER 3: HOURLY

The ADHD brain struggles to self-regulate and to focus in from a large field of options down to a narrow, single choice. That means the ultimate feat in task management is laying out your goals hour by hour, pinning tasks to specific times or blocks of time during your day. The logic behind hourly planning is that if you reduce your mind's need for in-the-moment decision-making, you're more likely to stay on task.

To work with Tier 3, you must keep your Tier 2 list in front of you while you figure out how to best lay out the day's workflow. When using my spreadsheet system, I tend to copy the respective Tier 2 list and paste it into the Tier 3 tab so I can be sure all items are included. If I'm feeling up to it, I will even jot down a range of how long I think each task will take, giving me a better sense of how to schedule the tasks throughout the day.

TIME	ACTIVITIES/TASKS/FOCUS	TIME	ACTIVITIES/TASKS/FOCUS
7:00 a.m.	AM Routine	3:00 p.m.	Start Up Proposal
7:15 a.m.		3:15 p.m.	
7:30 a.m.		3:30 p.m.	
7:45 a.m.		3:45 p.m.	
8:00 a.m.		4:00 p.m.	
8:15 a.m.		4:15 p.m.	
8:30 a.m.		4:30 p.m.	
8:45 a.m.		4:45 p.m.	
9:00 a.m.	Pay Amex, Client X Proposal	5:00 p.m.	
9:15 a.m.	Respond to 10 Emails	5:15 p.m.	
9:30 a.m.		5:30 p.m.	Grocery Shopping
9:45 a.m.		5:45 p.m.	
10:00 a.m.		6:00 p.m.	
10:15 a.m.		6:15 p.m.	
10:30 a.m.		6:30 p.m.	
10:45 a.m.		6:45 p.m.	Exercise
11:00 a.m.		7:00 p.m.	
11:15 a.m.		7:15 p.m.	
11:30 a.m.	Mngr Mtg Prep, Call Oven Warranty	7:30 p.m.	
11:45 a.m.	Call Jon	7:45 p.m.	
12:00 p.m.		8:00 p.m.	Dinner with Friends
12:15 p.m.		8:15 p.m.	
12:30 p.m.		8:30 p.m.	
12:45 p.m.	Make 5 Sales Calls, Call Grandma	8:45 p.m.	
1:00 p.m.		9:00 p.m.	
1:15 p.m.		9:15 p.m.	
1:30 p.m.		9:30 p.m.	
1:45 p.m.		9:45 p.m.	
2:00 p.m.		10:00 p.m.	Work on Tier 2 & 3 for Tomorrow
2:15 p.m.	Lunch	10:15 p.m.	
2:30 p.m.		10:30 p.m.	
2:45 p.m.		10:45 p.m.	

ENTERED?	SAMPLE TASKS	TIME (MINS)
yes	1. Pay Amex	5–10
yes	2. F/U Client X Proposal	45–60
yes	3. Call Jon	10–20
yes	4. Prep for Manager Mtg	30–45
yes	5. Finish Startup Proposal	90–120
yes	6. Call Re Oven Warranty	15–25
yes	7. Make 5 Sales Calls	60–75
yes	9. Grocery Shopping	30–45
yes	10. Respond to 10 Old Emails	30–45
yes	11. Call Grandma	10

If you can manage to develop the habit of funneling your weekly task list down to daily and then to the Tier 3 hour-by-hour view, you are *significantly* increasing the probability of reaching the 80-is-the-new-100 level of achievement. Yes, task lists are a commitment. Yes, setting up a weekly or biweekly master list is intimidating. Committing to look at this list every day to create a daily list is fraught with resistance. But it's a commitment with immense benefits for adults with ADHD.

Blocks, Groups, and Buffers

The three key elements that make Tier 3's hourly system work are time **blocks**, task **groups**, and transition **buffers**. As I look at my day, I create blocks of time that lend themselves to my day's goals, inclusive of whatever blackout or set appointments I already have in place. As I create the time blocks, I consider what group of tasks would best fit a particular time block. Finally, I try to build in fifteen-to-thirty-minute buffers between each block of time.

While I provide my 3-Tier spreadsheet to clients to try this system out, you can just as easily use a notebook, blank sheet of paper, index card, or other canvas to work this out. In simplest form, it would look like this:

- 7:00–8:30 a.m.: Morning routine (i.e., wake up, brush teeth, shower, meditate, eat breakfast, etc.)
- 9:00–10:45 a.m.: Call Alice, pay Amex, respond to seven to ten emails, draft new client proposal
- 11:00–11:45 a.m.: Review comments on grant proposal, call electrician re: doorbell
- 12:15–12:45 p.m.: Lunch

- 1:00–2:15 p.m.: Draft memo, set appointment with Hugh, begin bookkeeping reconciliation
- 2:30–4:30 p.m.: Team meeting
- 5:00–6:15 p.m.: Log daily hours, send team meeting notes, call dog walker, clear up workstation
- 6:45–7:30 p.m.: Exercise
- 8:00–9:30 p.m.: Dinner with friends

The blocks of time are as flexible as you want, and for many of you will likely change with each day. For others whose lives have "prebuilt" structure such as college courses, steady appointments, or a work life with many blackout periods, you would reflect those set time blocks and be sure to capture the few open spaces in your day and have a Tier 3 plan in place.

The buffers are "downtime" that help reduce burnout or give you extra time, if necessary, to complete tasks. People with ADHD often underestimate how long it will take to get something done. Buffers allow you to finish a task whose time you underestimated, or do tasks that you were unable to complete earlier or skipped in a previous time frame.

As for grouping, notice that I listed multiple tasks in each block of time. I may get all four tasks done, since I've narrowed my options. But I might not. And since 80 is the new 100, that will be OK. Listing a few tasks into a narrow time frame gives my ADHD mind a brief burst of pressure, since I now have to make a choice if I opt not to do something. This may sound counterproductive, but it's the kind of mind hack that works by creating stimulation while still allowing me to choose.

3-TIER TASK MANAGEMENT: PULLING IT ALL TOGETHER

Now let's dig deeper into the 3-Tier planning process. Let's say your Tier 1 bird's-eye view is open and ready for Sunday evening week-ahead planning. You can see your potential tasks all together as on a dashboard—whether that's an actual digital dashboard, a spreadsheet, a blank planner, or index cards on the table. As stated earlier, the expectation is not that *all* items listed in Tier 1 will be completed in a single week; rather, this view gives you a sense of what lies ahead, for this week and beyond.

Now, looking at Tier 2 and the week ahead, you'll pull tasks down from Tier 1 into the specific days you feel you can realistically achieve them.

You might have a dentist appointment on Monday, so you put it on your Monday list. You may need to call the plumber, and you put that on the Wednesday list because you know you'll have a bit of time on your hands that day to deal with that. If you're writing a book, perhaps you'll write a draft of one chapter on Monday and the next chapter on Tuesday. If studying for finals, you might split up the material across a few days on Tier 2.

As you move through the week, break each task down into subtasks that will help you tackle them, and arrange them into an hourly plan on Tier 3. Check off each task as you complete it, remembering at the end of the day that 80 percent is the new 100 percent.

Without an organizational list, you might and probably will still get things done. But because you can't specifically quantify how much you got done, you might conclude, "Although I got a few things done, it wasn't enough, because there are all these other things that still need to get done. I may as well have done nothing at all." Then you'll end up feeling dejected, anxious, and depressed.

Having a daily list allows you to check off the nine tasks out of fifteen listed you actually did. If you prefer to put a gold star or smiley face next to the items you got done, rather than a check-mark, go right ahead! Seeing them done at the end of the day will give you a dopamine rush. You may have not gotten everything done, but you've done a lot.

For the tasks that are left, simply circle them and place them on another day of the week. When the week is over, I refer back to what didn't get done that week and be sure they're included in next week's Tier 1 view, and the loop starts over again. I tend to work on refreshing my 3 Tiers on Sunday evenings, which I view as the batter's box for the week ahead. The tension for what's next is in close view, yet I am safe from the adrenaline-heavy dread of Monday morning's first pitch. This "batter's box" differs for each of us and can even shift by week—what's most important is to keep an eye out for that window and commit to refreshing your *3-Tier System* in time to reap its rewards of increased probability of success.

The key feeling here is starting fresh. This helps keep you aware of the tasks that you need to get done so that they don't slip out of sight and out of mind into the "not now" category, never to be heard from again.

Another benefit of the review process is to help you to see trends. Which tasks have stayed on the list for five weeks and not gotten done at all? Perhaps you need to reexamine whether you really need to do these tasks. If they do need to be done, what could you do to increase the probability of success? Rehashing and recycling your Tier 1 each week increases the probability that you will—eventually, successfully—complete those tasks that really need to be completed.

MAKING THE *3-TIER SYSTEM* YOUR OWN

Instead of looking at your Thursday task list as fifteen things to do that day, the 3-Tier System gives you blocks of time with manageable choices. But not everyone wants to use a spreadsheet or work on an hourly basis. While the next chapter will cover time-management tools in more depth, it's worth mentioning now that there are a number of ways to use this system with whatever planner or blocks of time you prefer.

When I plan with three-by-five index cards, I visualize the time separately from the task. On the blank side of the card, I list the things that need to get done that day. On the lined side, I write out hour-by-hour goals. These goals can then get transferred to my digital calendar.

Digital calendars may not be your top choice, but they have the advantage of sending you reminders, which are crucial for task management. When I say reminders, I don't mean just one reminder. I like to set three reminders: one at the time a task is due, one an hour or two beforehand, and one some time in advance. This keeps the task firmly in the "now" rather than the "not now" zone, reminding me of the ongoing passage of time.

A digital calendar also allows me to invite other people to whatever tasks they are involved with or affected by. When I create a writing session, I invite my wife, not because she's going to participate, but so she knows I've set that time aside to work on an article or chapter. This also creates a small degree of accountability with somebody other than myself, increasing my likelihood of achieving the task.

Even if you prefer fewer reminders or a looser schedule, you can still apply the concepts of the 3-Tiers System to visualize your tasks and make them feel more accessible. Using the system at all three levels allows you to operate as efficiently as possible. Just be sure to expand the bull's-eye, stay aware of the "now" vs the "not now," and organize your tasks in a way that increases your probability of success rather than emphasizing perfection.

Chapter 11

Time Is Energy
and Vice Versa

One of my patients used to like to say, "I have all the time in the world." That feeling is a huge trap that adults with ADHD fall into.

Task management and time management are interrelated. But the relationship to time, and the energy bursts and burnouts that often happen over the course of a day, demand their own examination and consideration, as do behavioral strategies for better managing both time and energy.

ALL THE TIME IN THE WORLD

The "I have all the time in the world" mindset is a Trojan horse. It sneaks into the psyches of adults with ADHD, convincing us we're strong and invincible, because we absolutely have the time to accomplish whatever our current mission is. But in reality, we've now smuggled one of procrastination's greatest weapons into our mindsets—and procrastination is the mortal enemy of those with ADHD.

At first, it feels good to see all of that time and how much we can get done in it. It feels like we've got it taken care of, like we have a handle on the chaos.

But the attack is coming.

The hidden enemy inside of this statement is time itself. Eventually, it's going to sneak up on us, catch us by surprise, and leave us feeling defeated yet again. Without a plan for task management and a way to track time, the pleasure that "all the time in the world" gives us at first a sense of false comfort and nothing more.

This thought process also reduces and redirects the pressure we might otherwise feel to get things done. We convince ourselves that we'll most certainly accomplish whatever tasks are before us sooner rather than later—"After all, I have all the time in the world."

Inevitably and before we know it, we end up pushing things off until we're standing at a precipice with more pressure than we can handle, about to push us over.

Between the "now" and "not now," far more tasks get put in the latter basket, which then drops out of sight and out of mind until it's almost or completely too late.

People with ADHD push things off until they realize that they're in a rowboat at the edge of a treacherous waterfall. With a sudden jolt, they discover that if they don't begin to row, they'll go over the side and be dashed on the rocks at the bottom. Many end up like I did with Dr. Levin's final project my first year of graduate school: unable to complete tasks on deadline, scrambling to negotiate a way through.

Many of my patients tell me they can row really fast and hard when the pressure is on. They can meet their obligations without anyone being the wiser as to how much of struggle it was to do so.

But if they're honest, most of these people will also tell you about that one time or those few times when they miscalculated the pressure and demands they were under, were swept over the waterfall's precipice and smashed under the weight of it all. This can look like getting fired, having marital difficulties, disappointing their children, battling financial repercussions, or worse. They ultimately become trigger points for shame, guilt, depression, and more.

HOW TIME GETS AWAY FROM US

Dr. Russell Barkley talks about the "temporal myopia," or time blindness that keeps us from managing time and tasks well. This blindness—or more accurately nearsightedness—results in a difficulty sustaining the "long view" of things. Where a neurotypical can see things on the horizon and hold that awareness in mind, those with ADHD see what's in the distance briefly, but then it drops out of sight until that event, thought, or obligation shows up again in their immediate purview.

Barkley describes such difficulties within and across time as resulting in serious problems with time, timing, and timeliness.

In practical terms, this plays out when we get a notice in the mail that a bill is due in fifteen to thirty days, and we stuff the notice back in the envelope, place it in the pile of other "to follow up" mail, and assume we'll remember or get back to it later. Or when we get an important email in the middle of the day and rather than respond, we mark it "unread," assuming we'll get back to it later, but it gets pushed all the way down as other emails come in and very quickly drops off our radar.

I might assume it will take ten minutes to draft an email, while it ends up taking thirty. My software engineer clients might allocate two hours to code a part of their program, whereas it ends up taking them four hours. The stay-at-home mom assumes she can cook dinner, do laundry, and manage her ten-year-old's homework obligations in a ninety-minute window, but it ends up taking three hours.

The examples are endless.

Why is time such a conundrum for people with ADHD? The executive -function system involves awareness of the passage of time and the ability to assess how much time it will take to complete tasks and assignments.

As a simple exercise, try setting a sixty-second timer on your phone, then close your eyes and see if you can match the passage of time accurately. It's wild how often my ADHD clients are off by fifteen seconds or more.

In part, this is why people with ADHD are notorious for being the last ones to arrive at meetings or events. We are chronically late because we struggle to get out the door and out of the house without delays—and because we fundamentally don't realize what those delays cost us in terms of time.

TIME-MANAGEMENT TIPS

Just as task management involves better handling our relationship with what we need to get done, our goal is to improve our relationship with time itself to reduce the amount of time we waste.

As we externalized our tasks in the last chapter rather than relying on memory, we need to learn to externalize time as well. Wear a watch and place a clock in your workspace, as well as other places where seeing the passage of time is key.

Dr. Ari Tuckman, a colleague from Pennsylvania who specializes in adult ADHD, specifies that an analog clock is preferred over a digital display, as you can actually see the movement of time in a relative sense, seeing as chunks of time pass through the clock hand movement—a far more palpable experience.

We can also externalize time by placing events or tasks in a digital calendar like Google Cal, iCal, or Outlook, but doing so is only as good as your ability to recall those events, so you must set calendar reminders—not single reminders, but two or three. These will make you less dependent on your unreliable internal clock and handicapped perception of the passage of time and more aligned with its actual passage.

Also, as we saw in the task-management chapter, focusing on smaller chunks of time helps us become more connected to the reality of its passing. People with ADHD also look for immediate feedback, which provides the here-and-now incentives the ADHD brain craves, and a focus on shorter time periods gives this a considerable boost.

TIME-MANAGEMENT TIPS

- Externalize the movement of time with an analog watch.
- Place events in a digital calendar with multiple reminders.
- Focus on smaller, more tangible chunks of time.
- Reframe your thoughts and words around time.

Let's look at a concrete example. If you know you need to leave the house by 8:00 a.m., you should set an alarm on your phone for leaving at 8:00 a.m.—but also place multiple reminders at 7:15, at 7:30, and at 7:55. These become external prompts that will help you keep the passage and narrowing of time in mind. Each external representation also provides more of the immediate feedback you, as an adult with ADHD, are looking for.

This is analogous to looking out for an exit on the highway. Multiple signs pop up in the miles leading up to the actual exit. The first may say, "Exit 11 to Albany—4 miles"; then again at two miles, half a mile, and finally a few feet before the actual exit. If there were only the first reminder four miles out, I may get distracted as the exit draws closer and miss it entirely. If there were only the final sign by the turnoff, I might not be prepared to shift lanes on such short notice and make the exit in time. Thus, having multiple "exit" signs promotes my capacity to prepare, stay on target, and shift into the required task with less risk of missing it.

To the same end, when planning to leave at 8:00 a.m., think through what steps you'd need to take prior to that in order to succeed, such as: at 7:00 a.m., eat breakfast; 7:20 a.m., get dressed; 7:40 a.m., gather your things; 7:55 a.m., head toward the door.

You don't necessarily need to write these out, but running through the steps in your head across that hour can help keep you on track.

As soon as you make a commitment to an appointment or other obligation, enter that event immediately into your digital calendar. As you do so, set your multiple reminders—again, two or three are better than one—in the days, hours, and minutes leading up to the task. Then, as we saw with task management, send a calendar invitation to any of the pertinent people involved in the particular appointment or obligation. This expands your circle of accountability and thereby reduces your chance of forgetting.

Another important step in our efforts to reprogram our relationship with time is to shift the way we use language to talk about time. Again, people with ADHD are significantly off base in predicting or estimating how much time it will take to complete tasks. Our overwhelming tendency is to underestimate how long it will take to achieve something. This has to do with increasing options and expanding the size of the bull's-eye of success. Adding multipliers to your expectations, such as giving yourself a buffer of at least 20 to 25 percent, accounts for that tendency while increasing your probability of success.

Rather than saying to myself or other people that my goal is to leave the house at 8 a.m., I'd say that I intend to leave *between* 7:45 and 8:00 a.m.

Rather than telling friends, "Let's meet up at 6 p.m.," I would tell them, "I plan on arriving between six and six fifteen p.m."

Not only does this give you a time buffer and expand the success bull's-eye, but it manages other people's expectations. Now it's a win if I arrive anywhere from 6:00 to 6:15 p.m.

If you think that working on your company's quarterly budget will take two hours, schedule two hours and forty-five minutes. If you believe it will take you six hours total to write a term paper, assume it will really take ten hours. You would of course then break down that overall effort into smaller chunks with relative expansion buffers in place.

Previously, my idea of success was narrow and strictly binary: yes/ no, win/lose, all/nothing. To someone without ADHD, it might seem like a silly ploy to simply change those definitions. But when 80 is the new 100—when close enough is good enough—it gives the ADHD brain a significant opportunity to feel something's been accomplished and the immediate-feedback dopamine rush that accompanies that sense of success. This is what adults with ADHD live for.

ENERGY MANAGEMENT

Everybody knows the saying "Time is money." I'd suggest that— both for people generally, and certainly as far as adults with ADHD are concerned—time is *energy*. In ADHD, energy tends to burn brightly but burns out quickly. Managing energy is as important as, and not unlike, managing time.

Living with ADHD typically means experiencing rushes of high energy when in a stimulated, hyperfocused zone. On other occasions, where there is a lack of stimulation, there's a depletion of energy that can even spiral into periods of depression.

Integrating a mindfulness practice that enables us to become more aware of these energy ebbs and flows and their relationship to stimulation levels can help in becoming aware of when it's time to tackle specific types of tasks, since stimulation levels affect the capacity for focusing on a particular task long enough to complete it.

I know that my energy level and focus are sharpest during two periods of the day: typically from 9 a.m. to 11 a.m., and also often late at night, from 9:30 p.m. to 11:30 p.m. I schedule the tasks that need the most focus and energy during these periods.

I also know that my energy drops after eating lunch, so I schedule tasks that demand less focus, such as making phone calls, during this time. That planning keeps me from staring into a computer, where I'm more likely to get weary and bleary-eyed, when my energy's at a low ebb.

This awareness comes in very handy in interpersonal situations. You might be able to give a heads-up to your spouse at the end of the day, or friends that you're out with, letting them know, "My energy level is at a low right now. I'm sorry if I'm going to be a little quiet." Under other circumstances, when you feel a surge of energy and stimulation, it can help to set the temperature for those you're around so they aren't overwhelmed. You could say, "I have a lot of energy right now. I feel like going out and doing something really fun. Are you up for that?"

People aren't mind readers. It's helpful to be able to communicate how you're feeling, rather than expecting others to be able to get a clairvoyant readout of your energy level.

In other words, time and task management also involve becoming more aware of your typical daily energy patterns. When is your battery going to be charged, and when will it be depleted? We'll be talking about mindfulness practice at length in a little bit, which will help you answer that question.

For now, let's look at a couple of tips involving communication around the needs we're learning to identify.

Chapter 12

———

Speaking and Hearing Clearly

Effective communication can be problematic for anyone, but especially so for adults with ADHD. ADHD creates difficulties in emotional and self-regulation, and these often manifest when we're talking with others.

People with ADHD tend to speak impulsively, interrupt others, misinterpret what others say, and lack sensitivity about what they say. We say hurtful things without meaning to or even know we are doing so. We speak before we think, saying what's on our minds, without filtering, which means we're often tactless.

Fortunately, there are some powerful behavioral techniques that can help overcome these challenges. Let's first explore ADHD-related communication problems, and then move on to what can be done about them.

SPEAKING IMPULSIVELY

A cardinal feature of the hyperactivity associated with ADHD is a tendency to speak impulsively. In a conversation, the non-ADHD, "neurotypical" person is able to listen and process what the other person is saying before responding. Those with ADHD are more inclined to blurt out what they're thinking before the other person has even finished speaking.

You often see this in meetings, classrooms, and at the dinner table. People with ADHD cut other people off midsentence. They feel that they must get their thoughts out immediately or those important thoughts will be lost.

Emotional dysregulation makes this situation even more volatile. Listeners often experience their impulsively spoken words as hurtful, insulting, or insensitive. If asked or confronted about this, the ADHD adult will generally express regret, explaining it was not their intention to be hurtful and that they spoke too quickly.

Here's an example. My wife and I were recently going out to dinner with friends and sitting in the back seat of the car. She was happy and excited to be with them and was telling them a story, whereas all I could think was how loud she sounded to me. Impulsively, without filtering myself or even thinking, I interrupted her and said bluntly, "You're being *very* loud."

She wasn't happy with me at that moment, to say the least.

Later on, as we ate dinner, the subject came up again. My wife told me she felt it was rude that I had interrupted her, and that I could have kept my opinion to myself. If I really felt I needed to express that opinion, I could have waited until she was finished or spoken to her quietly on the side, instead of impulsively blurting out a criticism that was arguably incorrect and definitely embarrassing for her.

Impulsive speaking often stems from a fear that we will forget what's currently on our mind. Our chaotic, three-ring circus of thoughts moves so quickly that we feel pressure and the urge to get out what we feel is a relevant thought before it's forgotten and replaced by another one.

DIFFICULTY LISTENING

Friends or partners of an ADHD adult will often comment that it seems we're hearing but not actually listening to them. Unfortunately, this is often true. Our minds are a flurry of thoughts and inner chatter that far outpace those the neurotypical brain generates.

When they're not impulsively weaving in and out of a conversation, the ADHD adult can often be found chasing down miscellaneous thoughts and notions that arise midconversation, taking them to distant places in the mind while the speaker assumes they have their full attention.

At times, as we'll see next, some adults with ADHD can actually travel down those mental rabbit holes while also maintaining a hold on a few threads of the speaker's content, enabling them to pull off a semiconnected dialogue without the others realizing what's happening.

Neither scenario is optimal, with comprehension and engagement suffering as a result.

To be fair, we really are often making an effort to hold on to what the other person just said so that we can process it effectively. We feel the pressure of having to produce a cogent and meaningful response. At the same time, our poor working memory often causes us to miss both minute details and longer trains of thought. This can make us appear disinterested or disengaged.

When we do speak, we often won't be able to stay focused and on topic, to speak directly and to the point.

One of my clients came in after having the flu, and I asked her if she was feeling better. A "neurotypical" would have said, "Yes, I'm feeling better" or "No, I'm still a bit under the weather."

Instead, my ADHD client delivered a monologue: "Well, I had this fever that just wouldn't go away, and it was really difficult because I couldn't watch my Netflix show and be able to focus on it because my fever was so distracting. So I started to try to read a book—I read this really interesting book that I think you would really like. It's a book about Abraham Lincoln and his battle with depression. And I have to say, I have been a little depressed lately. I think it's just temporary, and I'm really looking forward to getting back to my a capella singing group."

Multiply that by a thousand, because what we articulate is only the surface, and we have a picture of the ADHD brain in conversation.

JUMPING AROUND

A related but different tendency is when we presume that listeners are shifting along and connecting conceptual dots as quickly as the ADHD brain does.

We move rapidly from one idea to another, following patterns of association, going from point A to point X in under a minute. And we simply assume the listener is following along.

What's actually happening is that the listener hears an apparently half-baked litany of random thoughts, without having a clue about what we've intended to say. This is due to the ADHD speaker's mental cylinders pumping at a very different rate than the listener's.

At times like these, when you're speaking rapidly in what may seem like rants, do your best to read your listener's cues and indications:

- Are they following your train of thought?
- Do they seem lost or confused?
- Are they possibly annoyed?

Try to be aware of the pressure and rate of your speech, as well as your tone. When you get excited and are speaking quickly, you may start talking at a higher pitch. You may forget to take breaths between words or sentences. Recognize rapid-fire mode and when you're inclined to slip into it. You can eventually learn to tune into your body for the evidence and feedback you need.

OVERSENSITIVITY AND DEFENSIVENESS

One major communication problem that adults with ADHD face is sensitivity or oversensitivity to what we perceive as criticism or rejection (i.e., rejection sensitivity).

Again, people with ADHD are often lost in thought and preoccupied with trying to keep track of said thoughts. They may also be trying to control their tendency to speak impulsively. This means they're probably not focusing on the other people in the conversation as well as they might.

They therefore tend to miss the nonverbal cues that are a crucial part of any in-person or video-based communication. This often leads to misreading what is going on. However, sensitivity to criticism and rejection often goes beyond misreading verbal cues, since ADHD is generally accompanied by general emotional dysregulation.

For example, my wife might come home and say, with no ill intent, "Wow! The house is only a partial tornado this time." But I immediately and irrationally take her remark as an insult, an implication that I haven't spent enough time cleaning up after the kids, or that I often leave the house a disaster.

Instead of processing what actually happened, I'll react. I'll say something like, "How could you come home and say that? I've been working hard and taking care of the kids—so what that I wasn't able to take out the trash?!"

Now I've gotten very defensive and am ready for the stimulation of a fight, but my wife was just making an observation. Even though she wasn't criticizing me, I took what she said as a criticism and responded without a filter. It's truly hard for me to pause and process what she's actually saying. And that's just one part of what's going on.

The other part is that adults with ADHD have a lower stimulus threshold, and we crave that stimulation of an escalation. We need spikes in adrenaline and dopamine. So when someone says something to us that's even on the border of being offensive or a critique—or could be misinterpreted as such—we unknowingly jump on it as an opportunity to stir things up.

Combine this craving for stimulation with impulsivity, and the powder keg explodes—even though the person we're speaking with may not have intended to be critical or insulting.

My clients who are the spouses of people with ADHD will often report that their spouse has a tendency to start fights out of the blue or otherwise create interactions and situations that are intensely stimulating emotionally.

People with ADHD have a higher capacity to engage with drama and speak with intensity. They don't easily back down from confrontation and sometimes revel in it.

The irony, again, is that we tend to insult others due to our impulsivity and dysregulation, though we easily take offense to criticism and rejection, or what is misinterpreted as such. We can dish it out, but we can't always take it.

HITTING THE "SEND" BUTTON

What's true in verbal communication is just as true in written form, if not more so. These days, "written" usually means digital communication. People with ADHD are more inclined to send impulsive emails, texts, or WhatsApp messages hastily, as well as post and comment on social media without thinking the implications through.

The digital realm is today's primary communication medium, and this shift demands that you exert greater vigilance. When you say something aloud, it's eventually forgotten. When you type and post something, it's locked in, and while at times you can delete what you've sent, the digital imprint is never completely erased.

Everything said so far about the challenges of ADHD verbal communication could be said of digital communication as well. Moreover, with digital communication, we don't have access to the nonverbal cues that might give us additional information to gauge the appropriateness of what we're saying or the pace at which we're saying it.

With all this in mind, let's move from problems to solutions.

MINDFUL SPEAKING AND LISTENING

The general guideline for improving communication is to adopt a more mindful manner of listening and of speaking. But what does that mean?

First and foremost, it means to remember your breath. Believe it or not, breathing before you speak can make a world of a difference in communication. The general principle is to slightly pause and take a mindful, aware breath before your turn to speak or before sending a message. In both face-to-face and digital communication, remembering to insert steady, even, elongated breathing creates a buffer between your thoughts as they arise and the expression of those thoughts.

One way my clients and I like to think of it is PBJ—peanut butter and jelly, or Pause, Breathe, and Jot down. In this case, "jot down" refers to communication of any sort.

What you're effectively doing is slowing your brain down, giving your inner observer the time to do some editorial work. Consider:

- Is this what I really want to say?
- Do I want to say it in just this way?
- Will this be misinterpreted?
- Could there be a different way for me to communicate this thought?

The goal is not to second-guess every thought and intention you have. Rather, you're bringing a process to bear that can make you more confident that you're not speaking (completely) impulsively, and that you're applying an appropriate filter.

The pause and breath steps can be as quick as a three-second process, though longer pauses are recommended for more emotionally laden communications or on social media posts of a sensitive nature.

Another mindful communications mechanism is to observe your body while you're speaking. As you observe, look for clues about how you're feeling. Observe the tension in your face, jaw, and other parts of your body, which can give you vital information about the emotions you're experiencing while trying to communicate:

- Do you notice anger rising through your body?
- Is anxiety churning in your belly?
- Are these emotions impacting your ability to communicate clearly, calmly, and openly?

The more micromindful you can be—of your tone of voice,

volume, pace, and the emotional intensity of your words—the better. This level of awareness will go a long way in helping you appropriately adjust how you're communicating with others.

Microminding your body can also help you be a more effective listener. The goal is to listen as fully as possible, that is, to listen with full attention. Remain aware of your body for early warning signals of impulses to interrupt or give premature feedback. In both mindful speaking and mindful listening, the practice is one of being as open, empathetic, and nonjudgmental as possible. Remember to breathe and relax your body before continuing.

If you tend to overshare, you can acknowledge and perhaps apologize for this to the person you're speaking with. Say something to the effect of, "I'm sorry I just went off on a long tangent over there. Was I clear in what I said or what I meant?"

Observing other people's body language can also give you information about whether your listener is following along. Rolling their eyes, shifting their body, standing cross-armed, or clenching their jaw might all be signs that they're becoming impatient.

TIPS FOR MINDFUL COMMUNICATION

1. Breathe.
2. PBJ: Pause, Breathe, Jot down.
3. Micromind your body.
4. Observe body language.

HEALTHY CONFRONTATION AND REFLECTIVE LISTENING

As we've seen, adults with ADHD tend to become overemotional and confrontational in their communications. Fortunately, there are some simple tips to help curtail such negative interactions.

First, if you sense that a conversation that you're about to have carries with it a high probability of intensity and confrontation, it's best to set aside a specific time for such communication. Try to avoid such talks happening impulsively and out of the blue.

You might also consider setting certain rules for the communication. One such rule could be establishing a safety, time-out, or de-escalation word. If things start to go out of control, either party could say, "Flying saucer!" for example, as an indication that things are getting too heated and out-there.

My wife and close friends all know my flag-down word is "blueberry," and I can't tell you how many times I've been blueberried over the years! Upon being blueberried, I take a one to two minute break in the conversation, often in silence processing the conversation, before entering back in with greater perspective and calm (hopefully!).

This would be a technique you could use with someone you speak with frequently, like a spouse, a close friend, or a sympathetic business colleague. When it comes to the typical conversations, especially when there's a history of confrontation, adopt the reflective listening and paraphrasing technique to ensure that you are taking in what the other person is saying correctly and allowing them to be heard.

For any level of communication, try to listen with your full attention, withholding or inhibiting the impulse to interrupt and give a premature response. The reflective listening process is a simple but powerful tool to help with this. After listening to the other person's point, the first response is not to answer or retort, but rather to reframe or paraphrase what was just said to you:

I heard you say X, and that it made you feel Y, and it led you to do Z. Is that right?

This is a reflection that shows you're listening.

Let's take the interaction between me and my wife that I presented earlier. She might say, "I want to talk to you about how you spoke to me in front of our friends, because it really made me upset."

An ineffective response would be: "I didn't speak to you poorly in front of our friends. *You* were speaking poorly and were out of line."

A more appropriate response would be: "What I'm hearing you say is that you would like to talk to me about the way I spoke to you in front our friends, because it made you feel bad. Am I hearing you correctly?"

This gives the original speaker the opportunity to acknowledge that you are in fact listening to and hearing what they have to say. With that acknowledgement, you can now safely take the floor and present your own thoughts. Ideally, the other person would also use the same reflective listening technique before giving their response.

It can feel unnatural and awkward at first to mirror back what the other person said. But it does increase the probability of both parties feeling heard and helps each person direct their awareness to what is being said prior to giving a response. This will significantly increase the overall quality of communication in any interpersonal relationship.

Chapter 13

———

Give It a Rest

As we explored the symptoms and presentation of ADHD earlier in the book, we also looked closely at Techno-ADD. We considered its similarities to and differences to clinical ADHD, and some strategies for combating its challenges as our increasing dependence on technology exacerbates rather than alleviates the challenges of clinical ADHD.

This topic is so critical that it's worth a closer look, and it's particularly important to examine techniques for reducing technology addiction in greater depth. What we want to do is increase our control over gadgets rather than yield it to them.

CHANGING OUR RELATIONSHIP WITH TECHNOLOGY

Most people's relationship with technology is one of increasing dependence, and dependency is a notable characteristic of bad, harmful, and abusive relationships. How can we change our relationship to technology to make it healthier and more supportive?

The first step in doing so involves increasing awareness and recognition that this is a relationship. And like any real relationship, it is bidirectional.

In Chapters 8 and 9, we saw that earlier forms of technology, such as television (however influential they may have been), went in one direction only. That made them far less powerful—and dangerous—than today's "smart" technology, whose interface is bidirectional. Our devices, apps, and social media platforms collect data on every keystroke, scroll, and swipe we input, then use that data to continually adjust how they engage us. Each notification, badge, color scheme, and pixel is programmed with intention to keep our attention stimulated and responsive.

After acknowledging that we're now in a bidirectional relationship with our technology, the next step is to be mindful of the dynamics of that relationship. As in any relationship with unhealthy tendencies, we must understand the necessity of boundaries and limitations. Along with boundaries, we need to set consequences for undesirable interactions and rewards for desirable ones.

The goal isn't to end or eradicate the relationship, but to develop healthier rules of engagement.

TECH BOUNDARIES TO CONSIDER

- No phones/screens thirty minutes before bedtime—you have to give tech a rest if you want better rest.
- No phones in the bedroom at night. The pull for your attention is more powerful than you realize.
- Upon waking up, hold off on checking your phone/social media for thirty minutes. Give your brain and senses a chance to come online before *you* go online.
- During meals with family or friends, leave your phone off the table, and minimize checking. Be present and fully engaged.
- While driving, never text/type/search/engage with social media. It can wait.
- Do not stare at your screen when crossing a street by foot. Heads up, just for five seconds.
- When spending quality focus time with your children, keep your phone use to a minimum. They can sense you aren't fully present.
- Think twice, or three times, before sending messages/posts out when in an emotional (or inebriated) state. You can delete but can never fully erase.

BOUNDARIES AND BUFFER ZONES

A good example of boundary setting has to do with smartphone usage at night, and particularly at bedtime. As we've seen, the quality of many people's sleep has been affected because they're engaged with their smartphones or tablets late into the night, often on social media or watching streaming entertainment. This brings about an unhealthy imbalance that negatively impacts the overall quality of life.

One boundary we've previously mentioned is not to have your phone in your bedroom at night. Charge it somewhere else overnight and use an actual alarm to wake you up instead.

To take this a bit further, the last thing you do before you go to bed at night should not be to check your phone. Set another boundary by making a rule that you won't use your phone in the last thirty minutes before bedtime.

The same thing goes for in the morning. I've read reports that 90 percent of people check their phones within thirty minutes of waking up, and 60 percent of people check their phones *within five minutes*. Delay checking your phone, tablet, or computer until you've completed other parts of your morning routine. Brush your teeth and shower first. Perhaps wait until after you've done some stretching or meditation.

The underlying principle is to create a buffer zone for your brain before you jump onto your screens. Once you do get on your devices, the cycle of dependency—one might even say addiction—that is fueled by brief dopamine rushes, begins. Bring that under control by not giving it so much of your day.

By the same token, set some tech-free buffer zones throughout the day as well. Earlier, I suggested putting your phone into your pocket or pocketbook while crossing the street. This should be a no-brainer, but I can't tell you how many people in New York are bumping into each other, into cars, and even into traffic lights because they have their heads in their phones. And this is a time when it's both relatively easy and *extremely meaningful* to not be on your phone. Every time you cross the street, you should tell yourself, "I'm not going to be on my phone. I'm not going to look at the screen, because I have to be vigilant about what is going on around me. It's a safety issue."

For urbanites, which most of my clients are, another rule or guideline would be not to check your phone while in the elevator. Why? Because this limited time is one in which you can make a conscious, mindful effort to fight the impulse to grab your phone and check it—even though everyone else in the elevator is doing so.

During this thirty- to sixty-second period, mindfully acknowledge that you are in a relationship with your phone. In that pause, you're consciously creating a boundary to make the relationship healthier.

These are big-city applications of a general principle that can be adapted to whatever environment you happen to live in. If you commute to work, designate the time from when you park your car until you get to your desk as a tech- and phone-free zone. Do the same when grocery shopping. Set your buffers based on your daily routine.

One concrete application that will work for almost everyone? Eat meals, or at least one meal a day, without checking your phone. Crucial times to consistently separate from your phone are when you're with other people, especially if it's with your family or friends at dinnertime. If you have children, showing that you can release your dependence on your phone sends a very powerful message—one that will encourage them to take similar steps.

I have clients who set up a shoebox or similar box near, but not on, the dining table. When it's dinnertime, everyone's phone goes into the box—out of sight and out of mind. It's a lot harder to resist checking your phone when it's in your pocket than when it's in a box across the room. Similarly, when at your desk for work, whether at the office or at home during recent work-at-home shifts, place your phone in a desk drawer.

As soon as you physically separate yourself from your phone, you'll likely feel your body drop a lot of tension.

SUCCESS STORIES

These suggestions aren't offered in a vacuum. I've seen many clients benefit in very concrete ways from setting boundaries and establishing a better relationship with technology.

- A real estate broker, after removing 80 percent of his apps from his phone, found his productivity, focus, and sales increased dramatically.
- A client who was $30,000 in debt decided to remove Amazon Prime and was able to significantly reduce his impulsive shopping and get on a much firmer financial footing.
- A high school student who removed all games from her phone found her grades much improved. Another high school client who didn't remove his games spent over $8,000 of his savings on in-app purchases.

EXTENDING BUFFER ZONES

Now that you've built healthy boundaries into your relationship with technology with relatively brief buffer zones, the next level up is to take daylong vacations from your phone. People of the Jewish faith observe the Sabbath by unplugging from all technology, even electricity, one day a week. A tech-era byproduct of this practice is taking a weekly daylong vacation from everything smartphone-related: social media, work email, buzzing notifications, and all the rest.

You don't need to be an Orthodox Jew to take a weekly break from technology. Simply set up a day, most likely on the weekend, when you take a tech vacation, either on your own or with a group of friends. You may in fact find this easier to do when a few others are playing along with you. These periods of "cell-ibacy" can serve as steady reminders that you can live well and even thrive when not tethered to technology.

Don't take this break passively either. The point is both to set a day where you're away from your phone *and* to be aware of how you feel during that day. Notice what differences you experience in your body and interactions with the world around you.

Several of my clients have done something even more radical. They've switched off their smartphones completely and have returned to old-school flip phones. They've become "tech-lite" and can't stop singing the praises of this practice. They still have their laptops or desktops, but eliminating smartphones means that the level of dependence in the relationship has gone way down. You may not choose to go this far, but at least be aware that the option exists.

To take this a bit further: Do you really need to be on every social media platform? What if you limit yourself to just one or two nonwork-related platforms?

Each semester, I challenge my university students to consider reframing their relationship with technology. Recently, a student commented that she and her boyfriend decided to sign off from all social media together (Facebook, Instagram, Twitter, TikTok). Since doing so, the quality of their relationship increased, as did their grades, workflow, and general levels of happiness. It sounds radical to many, or like something you can see the value in for *others* to try, but you won't know what works for you until you experiment. Reset your own boundaries.

Pick any of the above efforts, from the simplest strategies in Chapter 9 to the more dramatic boundaries here, and see how it goes. After all, is your relationship to technology really the most important one to preserve?

CUTTING BACK EMAIL

Email flows constantly and tethers many of us to technology throughout the entire day. When you open your phone, there's always going to be something waiting for you, especially if, between your work and personal lives, you use more than one email system or server. If you're challenged with ADHD, this means that you can easily get stuck in the dopamine loop of checking your phone ten times an hour, since there will almost always be something there for you to deal with.

I highly recommend setting up "email hours." In my corporate consulting, this is a practice I see happening more and more often in work settings. For instance, people might check and respond to email between nine and ten in the morning, then go off of email entirely for a few hours, not returning to check again until 1:00 to 2:00 p.m.

Even if you're the only person at your company doing this, others will be able to work around it. You might set an "away" message during your buffer zone of off-hours to the effect of: "Please note that I only check email from 9:00 to 10:00 a.m. and 1:00 to 2:00 p.m." It's even more common for people to set up an "away" message for afterhours emails, such as "Heads up! I don't check emails between 6 p.m. and 9 a.m., so I'll get back with you when I can."

As long as you communicate clearly, people will respect and work around your schedule. In fact, they might even get envious of your ability to exert control over your email. If you can get other colleagues to do the same, it can help shift your corporate culture for the better.

PART IV

Change Your Mind: Cognitive Tools

Chapter 14

Think Differently

Cognitive behavioral therapy (CBT) is a consistently useful approach to dealing with the challenges of and fallout from adult ADHD. In the last section, we spoke about the behavioral side of CBT—changing our behaviors to compensate for the ADHD-related executive-function difficulties.

In this section, we'll deal with the cognitive side of the equation. This chapter will look at the way self-defeating thought patterns intensify the obstacles ADHD throws our way, and both this and the following chapter will focus on strategies for dealing with these issues.

EMOTIONAL STRUGGLES

Dr. Russell Ramsay, codirector of the Adult ADHD Research and Treatment Program at the University of Pennsylvania, speaks of ADHD as an "implementation disorder." While adults with ADHD generally realize what they need to improve and theoretically what they need to do to make such improvement, they have difficulty following through and implementing these changes.

In other words, ADHD is not a deficiency in knowing what to do, but rather in doing what you know.

However, even if you're making efforts to improve task management, time management, and other executive functions, so-called secondary effects continue to arise and impede progress. These include negative and pessimistic thoughts that lead to the expectation of failure.

Psychologists call these secondary effects because the *DSM-V-TR* does not list them among the eighteen primary symptoms of ADHD. Primary symptoms don't include difficulties with emotional regulation, struggles with depression, self-defeating thoughts, and battles with ongoing anxiety due to the hardships caused by executive dysfunction.

However, experts on and people with ADHD will say that these challenges are very powerful. Although they're secondary effects or ADHD byproducts, they're nevertheless powerfully debilitating. In fact, adults with ADHD often find these secondary effects among the condition's more disabling aspects.

Dr. Ramsay calls these "the ongoing corrosive effects of the disorder." The optimal ADHD treatment is multifaceted and deals with the whole person, and the cognitive techniques we'll be presenting in this section are crucial for addressing the emotional aspects of ADHD.

BUT THINKING MAKES IT SO

One of my favorite quotes comes from Shakespeare's *Hamlet*: "There is nothing either good or bad but thinking makes it so." This applies to everyone—but especially to adults challenged by ADHD.

Many adults with ADHD have had multiple experiences of failure or have chronically underachieved. Growing up, they probably received ongoing negative feedback from parents, teachers, and peers.

Such experiences can lead to the development of negative thought patterns that decrease motivation and increase disturbed moods and the tendency to avoid difficult situations. All of this reinforces the cycle of negative thoughts, making it less likely that an adult with ADHD will consistently engage in the difficult work of acquiring and using strategies capable of compensating for their condition.[31]

Grappling with ADHD involves frustration and disappointment, as well as conflict with others and within oneself. It's not surprising that feelings of depression, anxiety, shame, guilt, and anger are common among adults with ADHD.

This steady barrage of negative thinking gets baked into experience. Inner dialogue or self-talk often includes thoughts such as: "I'm not as smart as my colleagues." "I'm never going to reach my full potential." "I can't catch a break." "Everyone must think I'm inept." "My romantic relationships are always short lived and tumultuous."

The list goes on, but you get the idea.

Negative thinking is common to everybody. However, those with ADHD are even more prone to this kind of triggering. And they often don't slow down enough to take note of and try to combat the negativity.

This means that—along with behavioral changes such as time management and task management—working on cognitive restructuring to change negative thought patterns is critical to the treatment of ADHD.

The good news is that cognitive therapy, based on the work of Aaron and Judith Beck, Albert Ellis, and many others, has produced many techniques to help reframe negative thought patterns and reduce the related downward emotional spiral.

Negative assumptions about capacity, a propensity toward a pessimistic outlook, and dysfunctional beliefs can interfere with effective daily functioning. They can also get in the way of the ability to implement effective coping strategies by diminishing the grit, perseverance, and resilience needed to live with ADHD effectively.

Cognitive therapy challenges these negative thoughts and assumptions. The concept underlying this approach is a recognition that our reality is defined by our perceptions. What Shakespeare said bears repeating: "There is nothing either good or bad but *thinking makes it so.*"

Two people may be on a date, sitting over the same dinner, and engaging in the same conversation. One of them thinks the date is going splendidly—a home run! The other, completely insecure, concludes it's going terribly.

Two people are getting ready to ride a roller coaster. One can't wait, thinking, "This is going to be the most amazing experience of my life!" The other person thinks, "This is horrible! I have to get out of this line!"

It is the same exact roller coaster and the exact same date. But the two people's concepts of what's to come vary based on their perceptions, subjective filters, and earlier life experiences. Two people are in the same set of circumstances but interpreting it—and thus experiencing it—in two entirely different ways.

And a propensity toward irrational interpretations of external realities particularly affects the person who's miserable on their date or scared to death.

COGNITIVE ERRORS AND DISTORTIONS

The goal of CBT is to help people restructure their thoughts or cognitions in a more rational manner. The thoughts that most need to be restructured are known as **cognitive errors** and **distortions**.

A common cognitive error or distortion is the "all-or-nothing" thinking pattern, where you view everything that's happening as entirely good or, more often, entirely bad. For example, if during my pitch to a new corporate-consulting client, I don't get everything perfectly right, I believe I've failed. I'm a born loser if everybody in the room doesn't adoringly applaud after I've given a speech.

Another common example of cognitive distortion is the use of "should" statements. We focus on how things *should* be, which leads both to intense self-criticism and resentment of other people.

"I *should not* miss a single one of my child's Little League baseball games." And if I do miss a game, as I inevitably will, I'm a bad parent.

"My neighbor *should* have invited me to her daughter's birthday party." And if she didn't, no matter on what grounds or how justifiably, she's not a good friend or neighbor.

Comparative thinking is another cognitive distortion. You measure yourself against others, ultimately feeling inferior, no matter how unrealistic and irrelevant the comparison may be.

"The friends I graduated college with all have six-figure salaries. I fall short and am just not good enough."

"My cousin married an amazing person. I just don't feel like my marriage is as good as hers."

These statements about other people's work and marital satisfaction are based on very possibly false assumptions *and* have the net effect of making you feel bad about yourself.

Cognitive therapists have come up with lists of the most common cognitive distortions, and these lists are generally if not absolutely identical. That there's such overall agreement about which kinds of thoughts are generally distorted is a powerful indication that, however true you may feel these negative thoughts may be, they actually misrepresent the reality of the situations you encounter.

COMMON COGNITIVE DISTORTIONS

- **All-or-nothing thinking.** You view everything as entirely good or entirely bad: if you don't do something perfectly, you've failed.
- **Overgeneralization.** You see a single negative event as part of a pattern: for example, you *always* forget to pay your bills.
- **Mind reading.** You think you know what people think about you or something you've done—and it's bad.
- **Fortune-telling.** You are *certain* that things will turn out badly.
- **Magnification and minimization.** You exaggerate the significance of minor problems while trivializing your accomplishments.
- **"Should" statements.** You focus on how things *should* be, leading to severe self-criticism as well as feelings of resentment toward others.
- **Personalization.** You blame yourself for negative events and downplay the responsibility of others.
- **Mental filtering.** You see only the negative aspects of any experience.
- **Emotional reasoning.** You assume that your negative feelings reflect reality: feeling badly about your job means you're *doing* badly and will probably get fired.
- **Comparative thinking.** You measure yourself against others and feel inferior, even though the comparison may be unrealistic.

GETTING A GRIP (AND A NEW PERSPECTIVE)

I often tell my clients that cognitive therapy will help them realize they're overestimating a danger or difficulty and underestimating their capacity to handle the challenge. Even if your reality is difficult, it helps to develop tools to better evaluate the risks, dangers, or difficulties you're facing and to get a better handle on your ability to cope.

On many occasions, the propensity toward automatic thinking works against us. Just because I think something doesn't mean it's the truth. This may sound obvious, but our inner experience of our thoughts often ignores this.

If I drop a book, it's going to hit the ground a hundred times out of a hundred. If I knock on a piece of wood, it's going to make a knocking sound every time.

But then what happens? I'm at a networking event and say to myself, "Wait. If I go over to that person and introduce myself, they're *definitely* going to think I sound ridiculous. They'll realize that I'm a rookie or novice in this industry and that I'm not worth their time."

Because my brain just produced that thought, I believe it. I know it's true in the same way I know that if I drop a book, it's always going to fall to the ground.

My next thought might then be, "My brain just told me that if I walk over to that person, it's going to be an embarrassing experience, so I better not do it." Because I believe my thought, I act accordingly, convinced that avoiding that person will somehow protect me.

The problem is that our thoughts aren't always 100 percent accurate. We develop thinking patterns based on early childhood experiences, traumatic events, failures, and lack of positive feedback. As adults, we lock in on certain modes of thinking that become templates for how we view and operate within the world. And that limits us.

In other words, we're not really being objective or taking

quantifiable data into consideration when making our moment-to-moment assessments.

For example, at that same networking event, did I stop to think and ask myself, "How many times have I gone over to a stranger and said hello when there wasn't a lot on the line"? Maybe I have complimented someone who was waiting on the same line in a bank. Maybe I was at a ball game and turned around to say to the person sitting behind me, "Hey, did you see that hit? Wasn't that amazing?" In both cases, I got positive responses. Do I account for those interactions?

Most often, I don't. I discount these positive experiences or don't include them as data at all.

This means I'm not being completely honest with myself, and being honest is what it takes to give yourself a higher probability of making an accurate cognitive appraisal.

So what evidence do I have? There may be ample evidence that I've walked up to strangers and introduced myself, and they've received me positively. Of course, there's also evidence of times when I walked over to someone and they rejected me. You don't have to deny your difficulties, but you do have to take the full picture into account.

Another cognitive restructuring intervention is to ask yourself: "In case of failure, can I cope and move on?"

There's no guarantee that, if you go over and say hello, someone will engage with you. They may say, "I'm sorry, I'm busy." It may sting for a bit, but don't underestimate your ability to cope with rejection.

Ask yourself: "Have there been times in the past where I've dealt with rejection and successfully been able to move on from it?"

You might even notice that while you feel sure you have faced rejection in the past, you can't remember the details of the event, highlighting that what might feel "big" in the moment does not last in intensity over time.

Albert Ellis, one of the founding fathers of cognitive therapy, talks about this process in regard to his efforts to meet potential dating partners. He was so nervous introducing himself to women that, for years, he had never tried.

Ellis then decided to create an experiment for himself. He would consciously go over to women and try to engage in a conversation to see if perhaps he could ask for their phone number. (This, of course, was in the days before app-based dating.)

Ellis approached over a hundred women in efforts to strike up a conversation, and guess what?

He got rejected a hundred times.

But he persisted, believing that he should keep gathering evidence. The 103rd time, he finally succeeded in engaging a woman in friendly dialogue, and even managed to get a phone number and a date. So he kept on going, and his numbers improved. He was eventually able to engage and connect with more of the women he spoke to, to the point where his confidence rose, and he was able to reframe his self-perception.

Just because we think something about ourselves or the world, no matter how true it feels, doesn't mean it actually is true. With a brain that produces a lot of thoughts and emotions, we have to develop the ability to challenge our thinking.

Yes, we face failures. Yes, ADHD makes it difficult for us to rev our motor at the same level of efficiency as our non-ADHD counterparts. But we also have countless strengths and successes that we mustn't forget. We have many examples of when we pulled through. We have a unique approach and way of thinking that set us apart. If we don't call upon ourselves to draw on those successes, we'll stay stuck in a downward spiral.

This takes consistent effort, applied to one experience at a time. You can even search for the opportunity to practice: the moment where you notice yourself feeling anxious, angry, or afraid, pause to reflect. Ask yourself, "Is this the only way I can understand the situation? What would my best friend tell me at this exact moment? What would I advise a friend of mine if he presented me with the same quandary about his insecurity?"

There is more than one way to look at any scenario. If you can find these alternative ways of *thinking*, you can find alternative ways of *being*.

Chapter 15

Change the Frame

As we learned in Chapter 14, just because you think something, doesn't mean it's true.

However obvious that observation may be, it runs directly counter to the way many people, especially adults with ADHD, relate to their negative thoughts.

One way of beginning to take control over our negative self-talk is simply to be aware of it. The list of common cognitive distortions in the last chapter will give you a good start on identifying the kinds of thoughts that often lead—for no good reason—to the ADHD byproducts of anxiety, depression, and low self-esteem.

AUTOMATIC THOUGHT RECORD (ATR)

There are a number of different ways of reframing negative thoughts, some of which have already been mentioned. Asking yourself what you'd tell a friend in your position, as we just mentioned in the last chapter, is one of them. The tool I most often recommend to my ADHD clients to help reappraise and reevaluate their thoughts is a thought log, or an automatic thought record (ATR).

Our thoughts cascade across our minds so rapidly and automatically that we're barely aware of them as they occur. We usually tune instead into our thoughts' emotional repercussions—how they make us feel. An ATR provides a place to relate thoughts to feelings.

To keep an ATR, pay attention during the day to when you have an emotional spike or flare, whether it is anxiety, sadness, anger, or shame. Then record what was happening when you noticed this emotional shift. What situation were you in?

This description could include what you were doing, what occurred, and, if you weren't alone, who you were with. Then record the emotions you noticed. Were you angry? Sad? Both? Note what you were feeling, whatever it was.

Along with noting the feeling you experienced, rate the intensity of that emotion on a percentage scale of one to one hundred. This will give you an idea of the emotion's relative strength.

How frustrated or angry were you, compared to the most extreme rating of a hundred? Was it an eighty? A sixty? Assigning a number helps you see the difference in quality of your emotions. It also allows you to track when changes to the emotion and its level occur as you go through the ATR process. You can then report on and write down the thoughts associated with the emotion.

Not to worry: you simply write down the most prominent thought or thoughts. We call these automatic thoughts because they're experienced in a rapid, knee-jerk fashion. The point is not to write them all down, which would be impossible. You can have ten thoughts in the blink of an eye. Simply write down the most prominent ones.

Let's say that, among the emotions you felt, anxiety was the most potent—perhaps ninety or ninety-five on a scale of a hundred. Elaborate on what thoughts related to your anxiety.

CBT Thought Record

Situation
Where were you?
What were you doing?

Emotion or feeling
Rate the strength 0–100%

Negative automatic thought
What thought or image went through your mind?

Evidence that supports the thought	Evidence that does not support the thought
What makes you believe the thought is true?	*What makes you believe the thought is false?*

Alternative thought
Weighing up the evidence for and against, what do you believe now?

Let me give an example. Last night, I had a free moment just before the midnight deadline to submit my grades for the end of the semester. I noticed that I was feeling very anxious, so I paused to take notice.

There I was, at 10:30 p.m., sitting at my computer, with the deadline only an hour and twenty-nine minutes away. I rated my anxiety level at ninety out of one hundred.

There were also several thoughts linked to my anxiety, including: "How could I miss this deadline?" "I should have been more on top of this earlier in the week." "My students are going to think I'm irresponsible."

Now that I've captured the situation, the emotion, and the associated thoughts, the next step is to investigate the thoughts and examine how objectively truthful they are. Once again, just because I think something doesn't make it true.

Then, it was time to explore the evidence I had to support my belief or thought, and if there was any evidence that opposed or disproved it. Was there an alternative way to perceive the situation?

I had to remind myself that I had been working on grades throughout the week, but I had a lot of work to do in a short period of time. Delays do happen. I reminded myself that my students consistently provide positive feedback on my abilities as a professor and continue to sign up for my courses.

If I missed the deadline, I could email the class explaining the delay, offer my apologies, and promise to submit the grades as soon as possible. I often forgive people for delays, including my students' late homework submissions. It was likely that students would be similarly compassionate toward me.

But let's take the worst-case scenario. Even if some students weren't sympathetic, I would still know I was doing my best. I can't please all the people all the time. There's room for improvement, but coming up against a looming deadline is very common for people with ADHD. I was not the first and would not be the last to face this dilemma.

You might think I should have been working on submitting the grades instead of filling out my ATR. However, reframing my thoughts this way reduced my anxiety level from a ninety to a far more manageable fifty. I was much better able to direct my mental energy toward completing the task, and I did in fact get the grades in on time.

The goal of this process is to come up with reframed alternatives and more balanced thought patterns. The mark of success is seeing a shift in your emotional state.

This is an ongoing battle because we often have negative shifts in thought and emotion. Don't expect perfection from yourself in this exercise (or any others), or that you will eliminate all your negative thinking. Rather, the aim of the cognitive side of cognitive behavioral therapy is to give you another tool to reduce the impact of the downward spirals of negative thinking.

In the longer term, this process allows development of a greater understanding of your negative thought patterns. You'll gradually fall into fewer cognitive errors and, just as important, be more confident in your ability to recover when you do enter a downward spiral.

COGNITIVE TOOLS AND TECHNIQUES

These days, I recommend a few different tools to help my clients develop cognitive reframing skills. There's more available now than ever before.

Dennis Greenberger and Christine Padesky's *Mind Over Mood* is an easy-to-use, self-guided workbook that teaches you the ins and outs of cognitive behavioral therapy.[32] It also includes ATR worksheets like the one just described.

I also recommend Woebot, a cognitive-therapy app that utilizes machine-intelligence AI technology to help you recognize and reframe distorted thinking (woebothealth.com). My clients tell me it's been amazingly supportive. MoodTools and FearTools are other CBT-oriented apps that I recommend for basic CBT utility, with other apps being released steadily.

The obvious question here is how often you should do an ATR. As with developing any new habit, the more often you engage, the more likely you'll be to make a shift. I recommend my clients do automatic thought records at least five to seven times a week for two to four weeks in a row. At the end of the four-week process, you'll have begun to internalize this new way of thinking.

You're training your brain to respond differently to what are normally automatic thoughts.

Ultimately, you don't really *need* a worksheet or app to do this. The ultimate intention is to try to train your brain to recognize—in the moment or soon thereafter—that you're having an emotional fluctuation tethered to a negative thinking style, which ultimately impacts your behaviors and even your physiological state.

If you strengthen your ability to respond to these thought patterns with questions that draw on alternative perspectives, you'll be able to reduce their negative emotional and behavioral impacts. You can then reduce the cascade of negative thoughts. You can see evidence of a retrained brain.

If you can do this three to four times a week—or better, five to seven times—for three to four weeks, you'll increase your probability of success. Yes, it's challenging for anyone with ADHD to set themselves this kind of goal. That's where a tool like the Woebot app can help because it will ping and poke you to engage in the cognitive-therapy process.

CBT can sometimes be difficult to learn on your own. Books and apps will probably help, but if you find they aren't giving you enough support, you may want to seek out professional guidance. Sign up for a round of cognitive therapy with a trained CBT therapist—ideally, someone who is familiar with and treats ADHD.

A FEW MORE THOUGHTS

There's a reason our automatic thoughts are so ingrained and powerful. We were designed to think on autopilot because it's efficient and effective. One of our survival mechanisms is to not second-guess ourselves. I'm going to get eaten by a lion if, when I see one, I have to stop and think, "Is that a nice lion? Can I pet it? Maybe it already ate dinner and isn't hungry?" No! We survive when we react on instinct—or so our brains say. We just have to trust that when our brains say danger, we need to run with no second-guessing.

But the chances you're going to encounter a lion are almost nil, and most of our reactive, autopilot thinking does far more harm than good.

I'll add that engaging in cognitive therapy doesn't always yield an immediate shift in emotion and behavior. If I explore a new perspective, I may still feel anxious and depressed. But that's alright. The process is not necessarily about shifting every single emotion, but to be engaged in opening your mind to alternative perspectives. Just knowing that there are multiple ways of seeing something creates higher-level shifts.

If you live with ADHD, you're going to face cascades of frustration, rejection, and failure, so you're going to need to develop a stronger backbone than others might. The struggles will keep coming, but you'll now have tools you can deploy when they do. Whether they work at an A+ level on some occasions or a C- level on others, the tools give you a backstop so you don't slip and spiral completely out of control.

PART V

Mindfulness: More Than a Buzzword

Chapter 16

———

Cultivating Attention and Awareness

ADHD is an attention-regulation disorder, and the practice of mindfulness has been shown to strengthen and help regulate attention, as well as to increase emotional awareness and regulate emotional impulsivity.

Remember when I was in college and learned that my ADHD mind was like a three-ring circus? There were trapezes flying and a fire breather in the center ring and clowns running around and a guy in the stands yelling, "Popcorn!"—all vying for my attention at once, while I tried to walk a tightrope in the center of it all.

Since then, the circus of my life has only gotten busier.

Being diagnosed with ADHD didn't change my need for stimulation or cut down on the chaos that was and is my brain, and my life hasn't gotten any simpler over the years. Instead of packing up and leaving the circus, I've learned to control the spotlight. I have cultivated tools that allow me to direct my attention while everything else runs in the background.

I might spend time focusing on the fire breather, taking in the excitement and awe and appreciating his performance. Then later I'll focus on the popcorn, allowing all of the other noise to exist around me while I think about the smell and taste and crunch. I have become less overwhelmed by the chaos the more control I feel over my experience of it—and that control comes from a practice of mindfulness.

As I sit at my desk, trying to write, my attention inevitably splinters across a hundred thoughts. But if I focus on my breath as an anchor to the present moment, allowing my thoughts to pass like clouds in the sky, I'll be better able to direct my attention to the keyboard (and actually finish this chapter).

MINDFULNESS TODAY

While it has a history many centuries long, mindfulness began to get integrated into clinical psychology beginning in the late 1970s with the work of Dr. Jon Kabat-Zinn at the University of Massachusetts Medical Center. Kabat-Zinn studied Buddhism and mindfulness with world renowned teacher Thích Nhất Hạnh (1926–2022) and later integrated the teachings into a program known as mindfulness-based stress reduction (MBSR). MBSR was initially developed for adults experiencing chronic pain as an adjunct to traditional pain-management treatments and over time was adapted for general anxiety and other target areas.[33]

Since the launch of MBSR in the 1970s, other treatments integrating meditation and mindfulness strategies have emerged and are prominent in the clinical space today. These include mindfulness-based cognitive therapy (MBCT) for depressive disorder, dialectical behavior therapy (DBT), and acceptance and commitment therapy (ACT), among others.[34]

Mindfulness-based interventions use a combination of cognitive appraisal, mindfulness meditation, body awareness, yoga, and exploration of behavior patterns. Evidence has mounted over the years validating the use of mindfulness-based treatments for a wide range of issues, including anxiety, depression, eating disorders, and trauma. Recently, studies have supported mindfulness-based interventions for ADHD as well.[35]

These techniques are now used in schools, prisons, professional sports, finance, Silicon Valley, and the British Parliament. They're practiced in corporations such as Google, Morgan Stanley, and Aetna.

Meditation's popularity has increased steadily over the past ten years. This is due in great measure to the advent of a wide variety of apps, including Headspace, Ten Percent Happier, Waking Up, and Calm. With 36 million Americans engaging in meditation, the broader mindfulness industry has grown to $1.86 billion,[36] up from $1.2 billion in 2017.[37] This proliferation includes the advent of stress reduction, meditation and mindfulness practices within schools and corporations, and by influencers across social media platforms.

Over the past few years, neuroscientific research has amassed ample evidence showing the benefits of mindfulness practice, including improved attention, better memory, reduced impulsive behavior, and more positive mood. Physical benefits include lower blood pressure, a stronger immune system, improved ability to cope with chronic pain, and better sleep.[38]

A lot of misconceptions have accompanied the popularization of mindfulness and meditation. Although it was originally developed as a basic form of Buddhist meditation, the notion that mindfulness is a religious practice is misplaced. Despite its origins, the secular applications of mindfulness do not involve or require any belief in a higher power or organized religion. Mindfulness, appropriately, simply *is*.

MY MINDFULNESS STORY

As a way of leading into an exploration of mindfulness techniques and their application to ADHD, let me tell you how I came to integrate mindfulness and meditation into my own ADHD toolbox. In my early college years, I explored the practice of yoga by visiting various studios around NYC (e.g., Om, Jivamukti, Dharma Mittra, Laughing Lotus). I got fairly adept at the physical practice of yoga, but while doing the poses, my mind would race all over the place. It seemed like everyone else was focused and zenned out, while I had an eighteen-piece orchestra of thoughts, analysis, self-critique, and my grocery list clanging throughout each class. I kept at it, but never consistently enough to really lock in the routine or reach deeper meditative states.

In 2008, after hearing whispers about mindfulness as an emerging treatment tool, I enrolled in an intensive six-day certification in mindfulness-based cognitive therapy for depression (MBCT), led by one of its founders, Dr. Zindel Segal. The training was held at the Omega Institute in upstate New York, and we were required to start each day at six in the morning with a forty-five-minute meditation, with various other meditation and mindfulness practices throughout the day.

I'll never forget sitting in that room during the meditations, attempting to observe my mind amidst a cacophony of thoughts, bodily agitation, and the desire to blurt something out. The meditations across the first few days were nothing short of torture for me. However, as I persisted, I came to realize how rarely I had ever observed what my mind did for extended periods of time. Sure, I knew my mind was an orchestra, but to see and hear all of its happenings from a slight distance was a new experience. To take note of how my awareness quick-shifted between focal points while trying to let my judgments slip away was very different than what I thought mindfulness was "supposed" to be about.

By the end of the six-day intensive training, I had come to a new realization about the importance of developing a relationship with my mind. I had previously considered my relationship to my "self," but I hadn't yet done so with my "mind" and its constant stream of awareness. I was always looking at myself from *within* the self, rather than from the sideline, observing the happenings of my self/mind from a distance. I learned what it meant to purposefully empower an observer in my own head to observe my thoughts, while minimizing my judgments of whatever I noticed.

I actually felt calmer in the months that followed, was able to focus for extended periods of time, and saw a major shift in my overall emotional state. Within one year of applying mindfulness tools on a regular basis, and after committing to a Kundalini yoga practice (more on this in Chapter 21), I had significantly reduced the amount of medication I was taking and had a greater overall handle on my focus, mood states, and restlessness.

What occurred was essentially a rewiring of my brain through the regular practices of mindfulness meditation and yoga. It's been nearly fourteen years now, and admittedly, I do not have a steady daily meditation practice. I still have to fight myself to sit and meditate. I am no more zenned out than I'd been before—*and that's OK*. My newfound relationship with my own attention has enhanced my ability to harness my mind, my focus, my body, and my emotions, even if it doesn't look like the meditative practice I once thought I should have.

MINDFULNESS BASICS

Jon Kabat-Zinn defines mindfulness as adopting nonjudgmental attention to one's experience in the present moment. The goal of mindfulness is not to empty all thoughts from the mind. The purpose is not to tune out but to tune in, to direct the mind's spotlight of awareness in a deliberate way and notice what is actually occurring.

There are two basic forms of the practice: **focused monitoring** and **open monitoring**.

In **focused monitoring**, you direct your awareness toward a specific object. The object can be your body, sounds, food, a flower, a mantra, or other specific "here and now" targets. The most common and simplest object of focus is the breath.

In using breath as an example, the intention with focused monitoring is first to notice the target item, say your breath, and then to stay and play with that awareness. It's very much to be expected, and is quite alright, to get distracted and pulled away from this awareness. When you notice your attention wandering, gently invite your awareness back to the sensation of breathing. It helps to be playful with this effort, with the object being to be engaged rather than to "win." This can feel like watching a game of tennis, or better yet ping-pong for those rapid thinkers among us. Monitoring one's focus in this way can anchor you in the present moment since the breath by its nature occurs in the present tense. It's here and it's now. When you direct your awareness toward your breathing, you're essentially focusing yourself on the present tense, which is a key aspect of mindfulness.

Sitting with the breath from this focused, observant, and monitoring style for as little as *one minute* can be a very powerful experience for someone with ADHD. With time, you might push yourself to five or ten minutes. Every time you're distracted, gently invite your awareness back to the breath. If it happens 100 times, invite yourself back 101 times.

When your attention wanders, the tendency will be to say to yourself, "I'm doing this wrong! I'm a failure!" But whether you're staying focused is entirely beside the point. Everyone's attention wanders. The most effective next step is to let go of self-judgment as much as you can—practicing self-compassion, as we'll discuss in a moment—and simply return your attention to the breath.

The second mindfulness method is **open monitoring**. In this approach, there's no specific object or sensory experience to focus on. Rather, the intention is to be alert, open, and receptive to whatever you notice in your field of awareness. You invite your mind to notice and label whatever is happening.

This open awareness practice is an exercise in being comfortable in purposefully noticing whatever arises in the moment, again without judging what is happening. Eventually, you begin to understand that what you notice is temporary. Each of those thoughts, emotions, sensations, memories, and impulses is a fleeting experience, and you will have trillions of such experiences over the course of your lifetime.

A common analogy for this experience is the clouds passing through the sky. You could say to yourself, "I'm very anxious about…" this exam I have to prepare for, or this report I have to write. While each one of those anxious thoughts is like a cloud in the sky, you're the ever-present sky that will experience many different clouds. Each one of those clouds will pass in its due time and eventually dissipate, no matter how much they bluster.

In reality, *you* are not anxious; you're experiencing anxious thoughts. Just as clouds will pass, so will these anxious thoughts about the report you have to write or the exam you have to prepare for. You become aware that your individual thoughts and emotions, such as your anxiety, no longer define who you are. Open monitoring can lead to greater insight and acceptance of one's behaviors and experiences, and ultimately reduce the impact of negative emotional states.

MINDFULNESS AND ADHD

As an observer of your mental experiences, you are able to respond, with purposeful attention, to whatever you have noticed. You are able to simply witness and let go of the need to control the outcome. You're creating a space for greater awareness of what's actually happening in and around you, which is good for anyone, but has specific implications for adults with ADHD.

For example, it's easy to get distracted while performing a task and then think things like: "I'm so bad at this. I'm so stupid. I can't work like my friends do. I'm always being pulled away by my ADHD." But when you can direct your awareness to the present moment, you realize that, in this moment, you're having thoughts and observing emotional spikes, *and that's normal.* It's OK for you to have experiences that are grounded in and arise from your neurology, and there's no need for you to judge yourself as bad or a failure because of them.

Once you begin to develop a practice of awareness and mindfulness, the next step is to learn to hold onto it and control it. Awareness becomes like a dial on certain thoughts or behaviors that you can turn up to let more awareness in.

It took years for me to notice my leg shaking. Practicing awareness gave me access to the leg-shaking "dial" so that I could not only notice it and turn it down, but notice why I might be feeling particularly fidgety or hyperactive.

You might open up the impulsivity dial when you're buying stuff online or saying yes to things that you didn't want to say yes to. Instead of impulsively going ahead with that purchase or commitment and then beating yourself up after, your awareness can catch it and give you a moment to pause and come back later if it's still a yes.

Other areas of mindfulness dials for ADHD include early signals of distraction and being foggy, more readily noticing that you can't get into a thought or that you keep dozing off in a boring task. Emotional regulation, procrastination, and overwhelm can be brought into awareness too.

A mindfulness practice for ADHD creates your own board of dials. You might have a leg-shaking dial too, alongside an "I don't wanna" dial, an "Amazon Prime" dial, and a "What did they say?" dial. You may start with just one or two things that are in your awareness and then find that you gain a whole control panel over time.

ADHD Control Panel

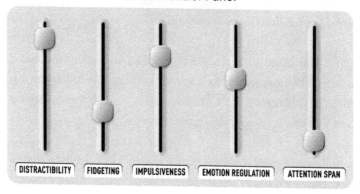

DISTRACTIBILITY   FIDGETING   IMPULSIVENESS   EMOTION REGULATION   ATTENTION SPAN

Ultimately, this practice gives you the option to ask, "What can I do about it?" rather than simply reacting. But you can begin by asking questions like, "What does that feel like?" "Is it in my body? My behavior?" "What is it telling me?"

Too often, we run our lives on autopilot without slowing down. Mindfulness just asks us to notice. When you practice mindfulness, when you direct your awareness with intention, you're able to tune into the present moment. To see what you'd otherwise miss. To give yourself compassion where you'd otherwise offer harsh criticism. Focusing on the breath or on open awareness enables you to become more aware of what's actually happening in the moment, and to minimize your self-judgments about it.

Importantly, gaining awareness about the experience of ADHD in your body allows you to work with your treatment protocol more effectively, especially any medication you are prescribed. Without practice noticing the subtle (and not so subtle) signals of ADHD, it's difficult to gauge whether your treatment is helping, what side effects are emerging, and what it might help to adjust. Bottom line: the more mindful you can be as a person with ADHD, the better you can manage it.

Chapter 17

Self-Compassion

Most people who live with ADHD will tell you that they have a critical roommate who's taken up residence in their heads.

Due to our executive dysfunction and emotional dysregulation, we're more inclined toward frustration, disappointment, and a sense of failure when things go wrong. Our relationships tend to be volatile. And despite our capacity for creative bursts of great ideas, summoning the focus needed to execute these grand schemes can be excruciating—which gives the critical roommate in our heads even more to say.

THE INNER CRITIC

We all have voices in our heads telling us stories about ourselves and our reality. For many of my clients, the voice they struggle with most is that of the inner critic, the one who tells you how worthless, hopeless, bad, and ugly you are.

As a kid who grew up on *The Muppets*, I can't help but think of this critic as the two old men who sit up in their box seats, carping at everything happening down on the stage. You might finally be feeling good about something happening in your life, when the barking laughter and jeers start echoing from the rafters. Unlike *The Muppets*, there's no laugh track to follow. Just you and your critics, wondering how you could go so wrong yet again.

Adults with ADHD have very real scar tissue around these topics, and a limited working memory brings difficulties that only make matters worse. It's harder for us to keep the big picture in mind, so we get stuck in whatever we're feeling at the moment and find it difficult to break out of that space. This cycle tends to lead to counterproductive self-sabotage. And that's all the more reason to cultivate self-forgiveness.

I'll go so far as to say that developing self-compassion as part of your relationship with ADHD is essential. There will always be bad days, which means you need to acknowledge your ADHD and give yourself permission to have bad days, rather than beating yourself up and stretching the struggle even further.

CULTIVATING FREEDOM

The goal is not to eliminate the voices, but to cultivate freedom from their hold on you. Much like we're working toward a better relationship with others around us and with the technology in our lives, we need to develop a better relationship with our critic as well.

Think of your mind as an empty bus that you're driving. As you go from stop to stop, you begin to pick up passengers, who fill the bus with conversation and noise. Some of those passengers really want to get your attention. They make extra noise, talk directly to you, and may even become critical of your driving.

Your job, as the driver of the bus, is not to kick the passengers out for making noise, or to turn around and engage them in conversation, but to continue driving the bus in spite of the noise. If you give them too much attention, you're going to crash. If you stop the bus to argue with them, you're never going to get anywhere. As a responsible bus driver, then, you simply say, "I hear you back there, critic, but this is my bus, and I'm going to focus on the road ahead. You're free to sit there or to get off at the next stop, but you're not going to take over for me."

Letting the inner critic know you know that it's there means becoming aware and mindful of its presence to begin with.

You do that by practicing mindfulness, such as open awareness. What's really there when we observe our critical thoughts and spot the inner critic judging us?

Natalie, one of my clients, had just finished her first year of medical school and was being penalized for being late with a couple of assignments. Her initial reaction was depression and anger. After we took some time to mindfully meditate on that experience, Natalie was able to identify being late as a byproduct of her ADHD rather than something she willfully did wrong, as her critic had told her she'd done. She now had enough of a handle on the reality of the situation that she was able to recover, not feel like a failure, and take measures to meet with the faculty involved and begin to move forward.

Natalie was able to examine the evidence for her critical thoughts, replace those thoughts with more accurate ones, and give herself the advice she'd have given to a good friend in the same position. Mindfulness and cognitive reframing work and play well together!

To revisit the set of *The Muppets*, mindful awareness builds another booth a level above the box seats those noisy critics sit in. They're still commenting and cracking jokes, but what you're doing in that booth is different from what they are doing. Not only are you noticing their criticisms of "the show" without identifying with them, but you're also mindful to let go of judging and criticizing the critics themselves. You're merely observing and taking note of the voices while continuing to experience the present moment.

Whenever you hear that critical voice in the audience or the back of the bus, allow yourself to think, "That's just me being critical and passing judgment." Observe and name or label what's happening. Then, once you develop greater awareness of the critical voice, you can apply different tools to counter it. This is where cognitive reframing techniques can be especially helpful (see Chapters 14 and 15).

KEEP ON GOING

Because ADHD involves difficulty with working memory, it's both unrealistic and unfair to expect that recalibrating yourself and clearing your emotional dashboard one day will carry on for the rest of the week or month. Your working memory doesn't hold on to experiences for the long term.

This means the practice of self-compassion needs to be undertaken every or almost every day, exhausting though it may be. Let me give you another example.

My client Alex was married with three kids and struggled to balance his work and home life. Alex was frustrated that he wasn't able to get a handle on checking his mail and paying the bills. This was one among several issues contributing to his marital difficulties. In one session, using behavioral techniques, we developed a system for him to go through the mail in a productive way, on a regular schedule.

After that remarkable session, Alex had a few weeks of success with the system, but then fell off the wagon and found himself back in an abyss of unopened mail. He even missed paying a few important bills. So we reestablished that the best course of action was to tackle the task every day in little chunks. Just as important, we worked on a practice that every day he would provide himself with forgiveness and compassion, realizing he was doing his best as long as he was making an effort. Alex planned to compassionately remind himself that he is operating with an ADHD brain, not a neurotypical one, which makes these kinds of tasks harder to sustain.

If you neglect to forgive yourself, all you'll be doing is adding to your emotional scarring, which will make living with ADHD even more difficult. The inner critic doesn't operate like most opponents, who head for the hills once you defeat them. Every single day, whether it's won or lost the day before, the critic is back on the bus, waiting to grumble at you again.

You have to put a daily, concerted, mindful effort into freeing yourself from the control of the inner critic. Self-compassion can't be overstressed here. Combining mindfulness with the cognitive techniques of the last section provides an opportunity for a more balanced self-assessment based on evidence for and against current, critical thoughts.

Sometimes the critic will be right, but that doesn't mean it gets to be in control. You may be having a bad day today and didn't succeed in reaching the goal you set for yourself. But you've had many good days, good weeks, and successful efforts. Having good days and bad days is part of having ADHD—and life.

It's a good practice to make this statement of self-compassion explicitly and even out loud: "It's OK if I have hard days and feel this way. This is a temporary experience. I'm not ever going to be perfect—80 is the new 100!" All of these techniques can bring the inner critic under control, so long as you remember that you'll need to repeat them tomorrow…and the next day… and the day after that.

Remember to be compassionate with others as well, especially those close to you. Adults with ADHD are hypersensitive and inclined to react to conflict emotionally. We can be critical of others as well as ourselves, so it's important to be actively compassionate both to ourselves and others.

If you do have a blowup that puts the critic or strong emotions in the driver's seat, first give yourself a day or two to let the dust settle. Then proactively address the disagreement with those involved and acknowledge you may have overreacted or been too harsh or too critical. Talk it through with them, and work to find the balanced perspective that you're trying to develop in yourself.

Chapter 18

Building a Mindfulness Practice

As an adult with ADHD, how do you establish a mindfulness practice both at home and on the go? The best way I can address this topic is to speak from my own experience.

To be honest, I've been exposed to meditation and yoga for over twenty years now, and I love both practices. But I still haven't been able to establish a routine of doing the same practice every single day. I could let my inner critic tell me I'm no good at meditation, but going down that path won't make things any better. What I can say, instead, is that what I do works for me. If you allow for imperfection and practice self-compassion, you can come to a similar sweet spot in your own mindfulness practice.

WHAT YOU CAN DO

For most adults with ADHD, the notion of doing anything on a consistent or daily basis is intimidating. Routine seems to be our nemesis.

If the foundation of dealing with ADHD is psychoeducation—learning more about the condition—learning more about mindfulness is the foundation of the practice. As described in the previous chapter, at its core, mindfulness is simply nonjudgmental awareness of the present moment, and there is not a wrong way to cultivate this in yourself. Reading this book is certainly a solid beginning, and there are ample ways to deepen that exploration such as through meditation apps, TED talks, yoga classes, or even simply discussing mindfulness with your close friends and family.

Small, manageable steps help us to deal with both ADHD and to begin a practice of mindfulness. When you learn that meditation anchors mindfulness practice, you don't have to do a thirty-minute meditation every day. Simply begin with three minutes. Or maybe you'll start off with a timer for just one minute. This also sets the intention that time in your day will be spent being mindful. If it's only a minute, it's a mindful minute, and that makes a difference.

> If you need outside motivation or accountability, you can also find meditation apps that start off with three-minute mindfulness periods. For all of the perils of technology, the integration of technology into our everyday lives has been a major vehicle in bringing mindfulness and meditation into the mainstream. A few apps that I recommend for developing a practice are Waking Up, Ten Percent Happier, and Headspace.

SLOWING DOWN ON THE GO

Setting technology aside for a moment (literally), you can also be mindful on the go. When I'm in an elevator, with my phone in my pocket as we discussed in the Techno-ADD chapters, I've got a good minute or more to practice mindfulness. I become aware of my breath or maybe, with open awareness, of the people or sounds around me.

It's not hard to find these opportunities. This is fundamentally about choosing to designate certain ordinary interactions in your life as mindful interactions. Doing so is known as applying "beginner's mind." Namely, approaching commonplace experiences as a novice who is still curious and open-minded. With beginner's mind, we experience newness and appreciation for what we otherwise took for granted, boosting our sense of well-being.

Eating is a common entryway into the practice of mindfulness. In his introduction to mindfulness, Jon Kabat-Zinn gives each person a raisin and tells them to take their time and slowly, mindfully explore the various sensory experiences that eating a raisin involves. What does it smell like? What does it feel like? When you bite into it, what's the experience of the texture and flavor?

That doesn't have to take place in a formal mindful-eating practice. It's something you can do before and during your first sip of coffee in the morning. Take a moment and slowly notice the smell of the coffee. Then notice the heat and taste of the first sip.

If raisins and coffee aren't your thing, slow down and break out of autopilot when eating a slice of pizza—which we all know can go down quick if we're eating on autopilot.

I look at developing mindfulness as an experiment, where I can try out different things to see what brings me into the moment. I might switch my watch from my left to my right hand and see if that helps me break out of autopilot and tap into beginner's mind when I want to know what time it is. Every now and then I use brushing my teeth as an opportunity for mindfulness, slowing the process down with beginner's mind, taking note of the sensations and movements, perhaps even switching to my nondominant hand to enhance the novelty. Such tricks build neural pathways to new behaviors and new behavior patterns. People with ADHD are prone to doing things rapidly, so just finding a moment to slow down and take the effort to be mindful can go a long way.

A WAY THAT WORKS

The inner critic never lets up. If I had a nickel for every time it told me, "How could you write a book to help adults with ADHD develop a daily mindfulness practice, when you don't do it yourself?!"

My response should be simple: "That's alright. I don't have to be perfect. I'm trying to develop mindfulness in a way that works for me."

Yes, it would be great to delve into a steady, consistent meditation practice. But if that's too challenging for you at this stage in your life, be compassionate with yourself and find other ways of implementing mindfulness. Just don't give up completely.

For example, in 2018, I gave myself the challenge of meditating for forty days in a row, but realized I needed a serious dose of accountability to make it happen. To do so, I let my limited string of Instagram followers know of the self-imposed challenge. I meditated nine minutes each day, naming the process Nine-Minute Sitts, then reflected on the meditation in a sixty-second Instagram video post. I was able to hit forty days in a row, but it was a challenge. There were many times I wanted to give up. I sometimes did the meditation at midnight or 1:00 a.m. because I couldn't find time to do it during the day. That was OK. Mission accomplished! I hit forty.

That experience showed me that, with effort, I could achieve a similar practice. Even though I haven't gotten back into a daily meditation practice since then, I still regularly integrate mindfulness into my life and meditate many days of the week.

Mindfulness has become my operating system. It's always running implicitly in the background, even if I don't have a specific day or time set aside. Over the years, I've experimented with and integrated mindfulness in many different ways and found the total effort is greater than the sum of its parts.

Mindfulness builds up over time. If you, as an adult with ADHD, keep applying mindful awareness in your life, you'll eventually reap the benefits of improved daily functioning, smoother interpersonal relationships, and a stronger relationship with yourself.

You can start with pieces of the practice that I have built, but find your own path to experimenting with mindfulness. If you can establish a daily, consistent practice, wonderful! If you can't, don't give up. Continue at whatever pace or level works for you, always working to keep the inner critic from taking you off your efforts completely.

PART VI

Mind Your Body

Chapter 19

Biomedical Interventions

Medications are the most common treatment used today for managing ADHD symptoms. This is certainly true in children and adolescents, but research does suggest relatively smaller usage rates for adults. My clients often ask about the possibility of managing ADHD without medication. I generally respond that, due to overwhelming research evidence supporting medication's positive impact, they should at the very least consider it as one among their treatment tools for living with ADHD.

MEDICATION: YES, NO, OR MAYBE?

The choice not to use medication to treat ADHD is often compared to the choice of someone with type 2 diabetes choosing not to use insulin. Some people prefer to control their diabetes through diet, proper exercise, and hygiene. While that can work for some people, the probability of success in treating diabetes is higher if you also choose to incorporate medication.

My intention in writing this book was to give adults with ADHD a 360-degree survey of the ways its challenges can be met in order to increase your probability of success. Medication is one of the many important tools in the ADHD treatment toolbox.

Since being diagnosed with ADHD, I have gone through years where I took moderate doses of medication every day and years where I didn't. Today, I use much lower doses occasionally and only as needed, perhaps two to three times every three months (such as when trying to get this book written!).

Some of my clients don't use medication at all, having developed the ability to treat their ADHD effectively with other life-managing tools. Other clients take medication every day. It depends on the client, what their needs are, and how they're best able to use the tools in their toolbox.

Tolerance of the side effects can be a factor in the decision of whether to medicate. For others, the question is whether they want to be reliant on a drug. These are all considerations that adults with ADHD need to explore for themselves personally— ideally with the help and support of a mental health professional.

You'll need to get a prescription for medications typically prescribed for ADHD if you decide you want to try them. I highly recommend that, if you want to try a prescription medication approach, you consult with a psychiatrist, psychiatric nurse, or psychopharmacologist who understands and works with ADHD patients, rather than a family doctor or general practitioner. This is specialized medicine and should be treated as such.

EFFECTIVENESS OF MEDICATION

Medication can bring about significant improvement in daily functioning in people with ADHD. In fact, research has shown average improvement up to two to three times greater than the results seen with psychiatric medications used to treat anxiety and depression. Research set forth by Russell Barkley shows that over 90 percent of adults with ADHD will have a positive response to at least one of the ADHD medications currently available in the United States.[39]

However, ADHD medications only work while they remain in the bloodstream, that is, temporarily. Afterward, their impact dissipates.

There's an upside to this for people like myself who don't want to be on a long-term medication regimen. I can take medication several days in a row and then reduce or stop the intake. Both the positives and the side effects of the drugs dissipate quickly.

In this way, I find medication to be a useful tool to rely on as needed. At times when I need to get a lot done but have little structure in my day or week, I might opt to take medication for a couple days because it helps me focus, avoid procrastination, and stay on task. At other times, when I'm doing well with task and time management, I opt to forge forward without medication.

Obviously, making decisions on general use and frequency of use should be discussed and vetted by your prescriber. It is not uncommon for prescribers to vary in how they guide patients, depending on the nature of a medication (e.g. stimulant vs non-stimulant; short acting vs long acting), a person's age (school aged vs adult), and symptom severity. Some psychiatrists might advise person X to take their stimulant medication every day without a break, whereas others might approve of weekday use, with allowable breaks on the weekends.

THE ROLE OF DOPAMINE

Treatments are developed by testing theories. As we've seen, it's difficult to determine exactly what happens in the ADHD brain to produce the syndrome. It's also difficult to say for sure why certain drugs are effective.

The low-arousal theory is now the dominant explanation of ADHD. ADHD brains are chronically underaroused because they don't produce as much of certain neurotransmitters, such as norepinephrine and especially dopamine.

The neurotypical brain produces dopamine to respond with pleasure or get rewards from certain stimuli. The ADHD brain produces less dopamine, which means those with ADHD are less stimulated to act, more inclined to procrastination, and have less impulse control. The brain has to reach a certain level of arousal to self-organize, self-regulate, and control impulses, and the ADHD brain frequently fails to do so.

To get a bit technical, recent studies differentiate between two types of dopamine. *Tonic dopamine* is the dopamine generally present in the neurons of the brain. Think of it as background dopamine. *Phasic dopamine* is the additional dopamine the brain releases when the neurons are stimulated. Think of this as the dopamine that flows and spikes.

People with ADHD tend to have lower tonic dopamine levels,

which leads to an underproduction of phasic dopamine. Much more stimulation is needed for their dopamine to rise to levels normal for someone without ADHD.

Since their brains are chronically underaroused, adults with ADHD are stimulus seekers. They're looking for ways to jack up their stimulation and increase neural activity. Looked at from the outside, this can appear to be hyperactivity on the one hand or inattentiveness on the other.

Two types or classes of ADHD medications work by increasing dopamine and to a lesser extent norepinephrine levels: stimulants and nonstimulants. Stimulants are far more commonly prescribed and used than nonstimulants, but we will look at both to gain a better understanding of what they are.

STIMULANT MEDICATIONS

The two basic types of stimulant medications currently available in the United States are **amphetamines** and **methylphenidates**. Without getting into technical chemistry, the main difference between amphetamines and methylphenidates is how the body digests and assimilates them.

The primary amphetamine-based ADHD drug is Adderall, although there are several other varieties as well, such as Focalin and Vyvanse. The primary methylphenidate medication is Ritalin, while again there are several different varieties with names such as Concerta.

These different drugs have different onset and duration periods. There are short-acting drugs and long-acting ones that remain effective for up to ten to twelve hours.

Why Adderall would be prescribed rather than Ritalin depends on the individual's chemical makeup and their body's response to the medication. There's beginning to be evidence that genetic testing may help target the prescription of specific medications, but this is still in its early stages.

SIDE EFFECTS

The positive effects of stimulant medications on ADHD include increased focus and self-regulation, among other benefits. But there are several less desirable side effects as well. A list of the common ones I hear about are dry mouth and teeth grinding, as well as reduced appetite, irritability, restlessness, headaches, and insomnia.

Another side effect I commonly hear about is what people describe as a change or restriction in personality. Without medication, people describe their range of emotion as being from one to ten. On medication, the range of emotion is more limited—from four to six, for example.

This is likely because medication cuts down the hyperhighs many people with ADHD have. To put it bluntly, it can make you feel a bit duller. This side effect can seem like quite an important drawback for people who work in creative businesses.

Continued use of these medications often helps dissipate these side effects. However, you should again consult with a psychiatrist or psychopharmacologist both to work through these side effects and to understand how to best address them. Your prescribing doctor may suggest a different dosage, a new medication, or supplementing the medication with vitamins, nutrients, or other drugs to mitigate the side effects.

NONSTIMULANT MEDICATIONS

There are also nonstimulant ADHD medications for those who either do not respond well to stimulants or have a risk for abuse. These include atomoxetine, clonidine, guanfacine, and bupropion.

In 2003, the FDA approved the first nonstimulant ADHD-management drug, atomoxetine (brand name: Strattera). Atomoxetine differs from stimulants in that it does not affect the brain's addiction-related reward centers. It operates by increasing norepinephrine, which focuses attention, and may result in increased dopamine as well. This medicine can show benefits in the short term to some degree, but typically can take up to three months to reach its full effect. Side effects, though much rarer than stimulants, include dry mouth, gastrointestinal symptoms, and headaches.

Other nonstimulant FDA-approved options for ADHD include clonidine and guanfacine. These medications can help to improve focus while reducing hyperactivity, impulsivity, and agitation. As with atomoxetine, there are some immediate results, but the full effects take several weeks to unfold. Potential side effects include fatigue, dry mouth, headaches, and dizziness.

Bupropion (brand name: Wellbutrin) is not FDA approved for treating ADHD; nonetheless, it is commonly used for adults with ADHD who do not respond well to stimulants. As bupropion is indicated for depression, it's often prescribed if the adult with ADHD has comorbid depression and can lead to reduction of symptoms in both arenas. As with other nonstimulants, some benefits can be seen in the short term, but the full effects typically take weeks to take hold.

NEUROFEEDBACK

An alternative medical treatment that's been explored over the years is neurofeedback, also known as EEG (electroencephalogram) biofeedback. Those undergoing such treatments have sensors capable of reading electromagnetic brain wave patterns attached to their heads with an EEG cap or headband.

The first thing the sensors establish is the patient's functional brain wave baseline, and the resulting brain waves are then compared to neurotypical brain patterns. Then the person being treated is asked to actively focus on certain tasks on their computer screen, such as following a fish swimming through the ocean.

This is accompanied by real-time comparison between the patient's brain patterns and neurotypical patterns. When their brain wave activity diverges from the target pattern, the fish might float to the top of the water, an undesired behavior. When the patient's brain patterns approach neurotypical levels, however, the fish drops deeper down into the water and resumes swimming around.

As this process is repeated, the patient's ADHD brain patterns are often pulled more closely toward the neurotypical. A feedback loop is set up that helps rewire the electromagnetic brain wave patterns of people with ADHD.

Some research has shown that these treatments can result in improved focus and sustained attention.[40] While neurofeedback for ADHD hasn't yet been researched in depth, momentum is picking up substantiating its efficacy.

At this time, neurofeedback is generally used as a supplementary treatment, alongside medication, cognitive behavioral therapy, or other treatments. Time will tell if research validates the use of neurofeedback as a standalone treatment with long-term benefits.

Chapter 20

Exercise and State Change

Research suggests that exercise may be especially beneficial for adults with ADHD. It both curbs symptoms and, by influencing brain functioning, helps you cope better with the symptoms that remain.

A 2015 meta-analytic study that incorporated findings of eight randomized clinical trials found that weekly aerobic activity in adolescents with ADHD had a moderate to large effect on tempering core ADHD symptoms such as attention, hyperactivity, and impulsivity. The exercise programs were held on average two to three times per week for fifty minutes over a five-week span.[41]

Research on adults with ADHD has found similar support for the benefits of exercise on improved executive functioning and reducing ADHD symptoms. For example, research has shown that exercise increases brain volume. The hippocampus, an area of the brain implicated in the working memory, which is often a culprit in ADHD, gets particular benefit from aerobic exercise. Exercise also triggers neurotransmitters, increasing levels of serotonin, dopamine, and norepinephrine, all of which are implicated in the symptoms of ADHD.[42]

Overall, research to date provides evidence that physical exercise represents a promising additional treatment option for patients with ADHD.[43]

EXERCISE ROUTINES AND MICROBURSTS

There are two forms of physical exercise I personally find useful. There are long-form **exercise routines**, which might include going to the gym for a full-body workout or engaging in ongoing sports activities (tennis being top of my list these days). I'm also a fan of doing **microbursts** of exercise during the day to get the heart pumping. Let's look at these strategies one at a time.

First, since adults with ADHD often resist routine, it's critical to find a type of exercise you enjoy. This may take some trial and error. Some people like to lift weights. Some people prefer to run or bike.

Many clients have told me biking is a particularly good exercise for ADHD because it can be highly stimulating. You're often out in nature, and the very speed of biking is invigorating. These days, there are also many stationary or indoor cycling approaches and classes, such as spinning, that include competition and rewards, which generally work well for people with ADHD.

Most doctors recommended regular **exercise routines**, twenty to thirty minutes long, three to four times a week. If what's usually thought of as aerobic exercise, such as running or biking, works for you, great. If not, use your ADHD brain to think outside the box and find other ways to get your heart pumping.

I generally tell my clients that to get the blood moving, you can do ten to twenty sit-ups, ten to twenty push-ups, and three sets of fifteen jumping jacks, then repeat as necessary. This will get your heart moving, break some sweat, and bring your exercise period up to the twenty-minute level.

What's also very effective for adults with ADHD, especially when you're distracted and need to focus, is to do what I call a cardio **microburst**. Just ten push-ups or a few jumping jacks will give your brain a rush of the dopamine and epinephrine to help you get through the next half hour of focused activity.

These microbursts also get the heart pumping and oxygenate the brain. They create a state change, from unfocused to focused.

But exercise can cause more permanent state changes to occur over time as well. As the research article "Emerging Support for a Role of Exercise in Attention-Deficit/Hyperactivity Disorder Intervention Planning" says, "This body of evidence suggests that exercise impacts structural brain growth and functional neuro-cognitive development, which in turn could have lasting effects on the trajectory of ADHD."[44]

SUCCESS AND ACCOUNTABILITY

Another reason I believe exercise can have a positive effect on ADHD is that, if someone succeeds in integrating an exercise regimen into their life, it provides them with proof of success. They've been able to successfully overcome an executive-functioning deficit and have organized themselves into an ongoing routine.

This isn't always easy for people with ADHD, myself included. It's difficult for me to stay committed to an exercise routine, despite knowing how important and valuable it is. During the weeks or months when I'm able to engage in that routine, the sheer fact that I have kept some level of commitment (remembering 80 is the new 100) makes me feel accomplished and self-confident.

I started out doing ten push-ups and ten sit-ups a day, building up the number of repetitions, and then adding a cardio workout on an elliptical machine. That became my routine for several months, conveniently completed in the basement of my house.

Starting small and doing something you find convenient are very important steps for those of us who struggle to get into an exercise routine. And don't forget to practice self-compassion! If at first you don't succeed, try again (and again). Just be sure, before trying again, to forgive yourself, acknowledging how hard it is to maintain routines with ADHD.

Aside from finding a form of exercise that stimulates and engages you, another tip is to find an exercise buddy so that you are accountable to your commitment. Perhaps you'll go to the gym with somebody, or you can simply check in with them and ask, "Did you get your exercise in today?" This works even if you ping someone who lives across the country.

When used properly, technology can give your exercise routine a boost. There are several web- and social-media-based exercise systems that also help to create a sense of accountability and shared experience. Exercise gamification also provides the stimulation and rewards that can keep you going. However, if you decide to try one of these exercise apps, again, start small. If you can commit to tracking even fifteen minutes on two to three days a week, that would be a great way to dip your toes in and see how engaging this tool works out (pun intended).

The final bit of advice I'd give about developing an exercise routine is to allow yourself to feel proud when you do manage to exercise, and express that pride to other people, which will give you a social-reward dopamine rush. Tell your exercise partner, your spouse, or another family member how excited you are that you just went to the gym and got a chance to work out. Reward yourself as much as possible until you get your exercise routine locked in.

Chapter 21

Yoga and Breathing Techniques

The health benefits of cardiovascular and similar forms of exercise have been recognized and researched for some time. More recently, the benefits of the more ancient physical, body–mind practice of yoga for health in general and ADHD in particular have been studied and overwhelmingly confirmed. In particular, traditional yoga methods of slowing and otherwise manipulating the breath have been shown to calm the mind and improve concentration both in adults with ADHD and the general population.

PERSONAL EXPERIENCE AND THE RESEARCH

Growing up, I heard my mother talk about going to yoga on occasion, but I didn't know much about it. As an adult, I first began to dabble by "yoga hopping" across various studios downtown when yoga was in its early trending stages in NYC. I was drawn to the practice, appreciated the flow of poses, and had a minimal resistance to the vigor in part due to my natural flexibility. Attending steadily and with long-term commitment, on the other hand, remained elusive. I would leave feeling good, would buy a ten-class pass to a particular studio, and would peter out somewhere between class four and six. Until the inspiration/guilt would strike again, when I'd try to get back in the rhythm, buy a new ten-class pass, and fall to a similar fate.

In 2006, at the height of post-grad school stress, two of my close friends encouraged me to visit a particular teacher of a particular yoga practice, as they felt it would "speak" to me. Alas, I was out of steam and "not nowed" the suggestion for down the road.

About four years later, in the spring of 2010, having then gone through a bumpy ride of early career imposter syndrome anxiety, working three jobs, and brushing myself off from the end of a long-term relationship, I grabbed my foam mat and went searching again for the yoga glow that was now in full bloom in NYC and around the country. This time, I was intent on working not only my body, but my ADHD mind as well. I remembered the suggestion of my friends to seek out their teacher, and that's when my big shift began. Before I knew it, I was rocking rhythmic yoga movements, vibrating along the sounds of mantras and gongs, and holding twelve-minute poses in a repurposed church on Christopher Street. Under the guidance of a wise and gifted teacher named Hari Kaur (HariNYC.com), I had found my way to Kundalini yoga.

Within a few weeks of ongoing yoga practice with Hari and other teachers, I was experiencing blissful mental clarity, longer stretches of focused attention, and became keenly aware of my emotional states and capacity for regulation. My mind and body were being engaged in unison, and I was finally able to observe my own mental and physiological experiences as if I was outside looking in, and then create small shifts from the inside reflecting out.

Something amazing was happening. I skipped the ten-class pass and signed up for Hari's two-hundred-hour Teacher Certification Training Course. This decision in September 2010, along my mindfulness-based cognitive therapy training in 2009, was a game-changing, "I Choose Door Number Three" shift in my life.

In brief, Kundalini integrates the physical exercises of yoga with intensive breathing and meditation techniques. After one year of practice, I reduced my medication considerably, down to an as-needed basis. I'm convinced I changed my brain chemistry and became able to exert more control over the state of my mind and its executive-function system.

The extensive research that's been conducted on the effects of yogic breath manipulation, starting in the 1990s and intensifying in the last two decades, confirms my and many other people's personal experiences. These studies measure brain wave patterns before, during, and after breath manipulation techniques, and their calming effects on both children and adults with ADHD have been confirmed. Beyond relaxation, yoga and breathing techniques can increase attention, enhance focus, and provide a cleaner lens for concentrated work.

This is also true of the general population, which implies that breath manipulation can benefit those suffering from Techno-ADD, as well as other forms of general and technologically induced stress.

BENEFITS OF BREATH MANIPULATION

Let's first distinguish between yogic breath manipulation and mindfulness of breath. Mindfulness practice often uses the breath as an anchor of attention. It does not attempt to change or manipulate the way you breathe, but uses the breath as an object of focused attention.

We'll now be looking at ways of manipulating the breath—changing the way you breathe—as methods for shifting the internal experience of your body and mind. Breath manipulation and mindfulness of breath are different techniques that complement one another.

Most of our breathing is what's referred to as shallow breathing, which occurs when we're not paying attention to our breath. The lungs are comprised of three chambers. The clavicle area is the upper chamber, the chest is the middle chamber, and the abdomen is the lowest chamber. We typically breathe only into the upper parts of our lungs located around the clavicle or breastbone.

When we're stressed, we tend to breathe exclusively into the upper and middle chambers. Our breaths are short and fast paced.

Upper Chest/Shallow Breathing

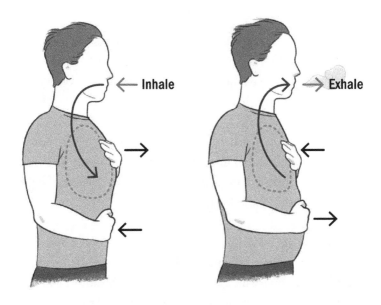

← **Inhale**   → **Exhale**

Most of us go through our lives with high stress levels. Our work-days are hectic, and our responsibility levels are overwhelming. We never seem to have enough time at our disposal, and we usually operate under strain. Under this constant strain, shallow breaths become normal.

Unfortunately, this type of breathing triggers the sympathetic nervous system, which releases stress hormones and elevates the heart rate, blood pressure, and muscle tension. All of this heightens stress levels, which causes adults with ADHD and Techno-ADD to react impulsively, have short fuses, and speak out of frustration more frequently.

Shallow breathing, at the "normal" rate of fourteen to twenty breaths per minute, is correlated with higher rates of panic attacks.

It can also cause problems for those who experience depression, as many adults with ADHD do.

Although it's common, shallow breathing is a less effective and efficient way to breathe. It constricts the blood vessels, which then supply us with less energy. The brain becomes less oxygenated and works more slowly.

Shallow breathing is associated with the fight-or-flight response, the state of mind we get into when we feel threatened. This was originally an adaptive mechanism to help us prepare for, fight against, or escape from danger.

However, if the body misinterprets the environment and concludes—for instance, when a deadline is looming—that there is danger when none really exists, shallow, tense breathing and the sympathetic-nervous-system domino effect are still triggered even if we know the actual threat to our well-being is minimal. Living in this state for long periods increases the risk of heart failure and stroke and is generally bad for your health.

Adults with ADHD who are emotionally dysregulated, have low frustration tolerance, and have high impulsivity are at high risk for these ill effects. That's what makes using the breath as a way of rebalancing and recalibrating the body so critical. It's vital for us to know how to use the breath to counteract, rather than cause and reinforce, stress and fight-or-flight states.

This occurs with Techno-ADD as well. People tethered to their phones also have high levels of fight-or-flight response. Smartphones are designed to send you alerts that make you feel as if you are missing out on something. They're designed to give us a sense of danger if we don't answer our email or check our Instagram feed.

The breathing techniques you're about to learn are beneficial for everyone, since we're all stressed and anxious, but they are especially important for anyone with ADHD and/or Techno-ADD. Decreased stress contributes to increased focus and reduced impulsivity, and breathing techniques can help introduce space in your body and brain that enables you to think more clearly about any impulsive actions you're about to take.

DIAPHRAGMATIC BREATHING

The most basic, direct method for balancing shallow breathing is referred to as deep breathing or diaphragmatic breathing. It slows and brings the breath into the lowest of the three chambers of the lungs located in the abdomen or belly. It also activates not the sympathetic but the parasympathetic nervous system, which brings calm rather than stress to the body.

The diaphragm is a large, dome-shaped muscle located at the base of the lungs. Your abdominal muscles help move the diaphragm and give you more power to empty your lungs. Diaphragmatic is the most effective, efficient way of breathing. There are many videos and demonstrations for this online, but we'll walk through a simple explanation here.

Diaphragmatic/Belly Breathing [Standing]

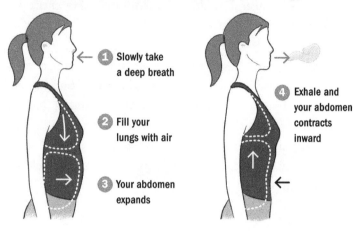

1. Slowly take a deep breath
2. Fill your lungs with air
3. Your abdomen expands
4. Exhale and your abdomen contracts inward

The best way to learn diaphragmatic breathing is to lie on your back on a flat surface or in bed, with your knees bent and your head supported. You can use a pillow under your knees to support your legs. Place one hand on your upper chest and the other just below your rib cage. This will allow you to feel your diaphragm move as you breathe.

For a few moments, just watch your breath, noticing where it is going in your body.

Then breathe in slowly through your nose so that your stomach moves out against your hand. The hand on your chest should remain as still as possible. If you watch a baby sleep, you'll see their abdomen is moving in and out as such, like a balloon is inflating inside the belly.

Diaphragmatic/Belly Breathing [Lying Down]

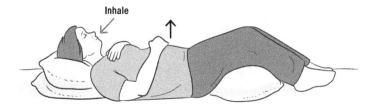

Inhale

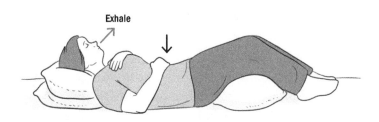

Exhale

Then slowly tighten your stomach muscles, letting them fall inward as you exhale through your nose. The hand on your upper chest should remain as still as possible.

At the beginning, you may find it helpful to actually force this action a bit, almost pushing your belly muscles out without even breathing. Just practice moving the muscles in your abdomen, pushing them out and pulling them in, out and in.

Next, pull the breath through your nostrils down into your esophagus, bypassing your chest and going right into the belly. Then blow it out through the nose. As you inhale, your belly should expand, and as you exhale, it should drop.

Inhale: belly out or up. Exhale: belly in or down. Practice this technique for thirty seconds or more.

A slightly more advanced version of this technique is called three-part breathing. Begin by pulling the breath down into the belly as before. Then after you fill in the belly, keep pulling the air into the middle region or chest, and then up into the clavicle area or top of your chest. You're now fully inflating the whole respiratory system. Then let out a slow exhale, allowing each area to deflate.

While practicing, you can try counting silently. You can count up to five as you inhale, hold the breath in for a count of five, count to five as you exhale, and then hold the breath out for a count of five. The entire process will take about twenty seconds, so you'll be breathing about three rather than fifteen or twenty times a minute. While you're just getting started, you can make your counts shorter: count to three rather than five, for example.

Try it now and see how it feels.

As you gain more practice, you can try the diaphragmatic breathing technique while sitting in a chair. First, sit comfortably, with your knees bent and your shoulders and neck relaxed. Then breathe in slowly through your nose so that your stomach moves out against your hand. The hand on your chest should remain as still as possible. Place one hand on your upper chest and the other just below your rib cage. This will allow you to feel your diaphragm move as you breathe. Tighten your stomach muscles, letting them fall inward as you exhale through your nose.

Ultimately, this is something you want to be able to do, in a modified form, without using your hands, while standing up, sitting down, and moving about your day. You can then do calming diaphragmatic breathing or even the three-part breath while waiting at a stop light, waiting for the train, while at dinner with friends, or before you start speaking at a work meeting.

BREATH OF FIRE

Breath of Fire is the other yogic breathing technique, very different from diaphragmatic breathing, that I've found helpful with ADHD. The Breath of Fire rapidly oxygenates the brain, promoting focus, and helps reduce stress by strengthening the nervous system. It expands lung capacity and releases toxins from the lungs and blood vessels.

The Breath of Fire is powered from the navel point, moving between the breastbone and navel, using the diaphragm to pump the navel in and out. I find it helps me focus if I put my fingers right beneath my rib cage and above the navel to become the focal point of both the exhale and inhale.

To do the Breath of Fire, first sit up tall on a chair or the floor, with a straight spine. Put your hands on your knees, or with two fingers four inches above the navel point, and close your eyes. Start by feeling your belly expand with each inhale and contract with each exhale.

First take a deep breath through your nose. Then pump your diaphragm quickly and forcefully, expelling your breath as you do.

When you then relax your navel point, you will naturally take a short breath in. You don't need to try to breathe in. That will happen by itself. Focus instead on the exhale.

Quicken the pace of the inhale and exhale, keeping them about equal in length. The full inhale–exhale cycle will be brief—probably a second or less. Repeat this several times—for as long as a minute once you have the hang of it—and then relax, breathing normally through the nose for twenty seconds or so. You can then do another round of Breath of Fire, then relax, and do a third round.

YOGA POSTURES AND PRACTICE

There's been a yoga revolution in America over the past twenty years, which has more recently been paralleled by a growth of interest in mindfulness. While a smaller group of people in this country may have practiced yoga in earlier decades, today it's a massive, multibillion-dollar industry—and for good reason.

For those of us with ADHD and Techno-ADD, yoga is an excellent form of exercise, because its techniques work the mind as well as the body. Yoga provides the benefits of both exercise and meditation in a combination of techniques that brings physiological, neurochemical, and psychological benefits. At this point, there's even yoga-based cognitive behavioral therapy (CBT).

There are many different forms of yoga, most of which incorporate a set or series of physical postures that include guidance on how to direct your awareness while in the poses. Your body is being exercised at the same time that your mind consciously focuses— the body supports the mind, and the mind supports the body.

This is where I've found Kundalini yoga to be especially helpful for ADHD. When you're in a pose, you're often instructed to close your eyes and direct your attention to the point in the middle of your brow above and between your eyes. Keeping your attention focused on a single point works to counteract the usual ADHD distractibility.

As always, of course, you can try different yoga approaches to see what works best for you. For me and many other adults with ADHD, Kundalini works well because the instructions always include engaging and focusing the mind, whether on the point on your brow I just mentioned, the breath, a mantra, or a chant. There's always something pulling the mind in a specific direction so that you're training it and the body simultaneously.

Yoga requires instruction, however, and once again, technology can help. There are now any number of smartphone yoga apps, online courses, and virtual yoga teachers to choose from. Face-to-face yoga centers have sprung up everywhere as well—there are probably several in your community, as well as yoga classes to take in gyms and community centers. It's everywhere, and I highly recommend taking advantage of this now extremely popular form of exercise and mindfulness practice.

Chapter 22

Organized Chaos for Body and Mind

Let's zoom back and finish up with a broader perspective, using a philosophy I've developed with the help of a couple of close colleagues. I think it applies to life in general but is especially helpful to those with Techno-ADD and particularly clinical ADHD.

This philosophy goes by the acronym LMNOP, and following these methods for living will enhance your day-to-day existence and help you deal more effectively with the challenges of ADHD.

KNOW YOUR LMNOPS

Most of us are fairly familiar with the ABCs of life. We have the basics down. We've learned a lot about careers, relationships, and the elementary steps of living a happy life.

But many if not most of us have yet to get to the advanced level of living, which I refer to as the LMNOPs. LMNOP is a philosophy for living a positive, productive, and engaging life, and it's built from the concepts we've worked through together in this book.

L is to *live*. To live, as we mean it, is to consciously be aware that you are alive and that your breath is part of your life. Remember to take a few minutes to breathe. Remember that you are a physical being that has this amazing set of limbs, muscles, and sinews that need to be activated, using an equally amazing set of circuitry in your brain.

M is to practice *mindfulness*. To live mindfully is to turn off the autopilot we're so often on and get into the driver's seat of your life. Become more aware of your present state of mind and body—your thoughts, emotions, and feelings. Be aware in and of the present moment, while minimizing and reducing judgments. Reduce self-judgment in particular by practicing self-compassion while focusing your awareness.

N is to notice. When you become mindfully aware, you unleash your innate ability to notice the *real* now, not just what creates stimulation. You develop a capacity for tuning in to what is going on within you and around you. Think back to what you've been doing for the last thirty minutes:

- Are you being productive?
- Are you focused on the task at hand or distracted by social media?
- Is your mind spinning over and over on the same thought, paralyzing you?
- Are you noticing a sense of excitement as you prepare for a big meeting?

Take time to notice what's going on. If you're distracted, close your eyes for a few moments and focus on your breath. Your breath is an anchor to the present moment; it can help you notice where you are and bring you back to the here and now.

O is for opportunity, which is what you are able to notice when you're mindfully aware. These may be business, social, or personal opportunities. They could involve insights about changes that need to be made.

It's not uncommon for people to report after their daily meditation that a new idea or a new thought has arisen, often involving an opportunity for change. With a clear, present-oriented state of mind, you can more easily direct yourself to this new opportunity.

When you're at a party and feeling down and distracted, it's difficult to notice opportunities to connect with new people. Mindful awareness, on the other hand, gives you a greater ability to connect with others and take advantage of the opportunities that arise.

P is to personalize your path. It's up to you to implement this fifth element. It is personal and, like a kaleidoscope of potential, can shift and change with your effort. It's the lens with which you focus your mindful living and opportunity seeking, and that lens is different for every person and can change every day.

One personalized P I find especially helpful is **pausing**. A pause can help you develop a better relationship with your technology so that it doesn't overwhelm, overload, or overly distract you.

Another might be **productivity**.

Some days are personalized with a sense of **playfulness**. Still others are personalized through **positivity, passion, poetry, painting,** and the ADHD adult's favorite—**planning**. (You thought I'd say procrastination, didn't you?)

This step brings everything together—living a mindful life, noticing opportunities, and pursuing the path that opens up.

OWN YOUR PATH FORWARD

ADHD gets a bad rap. As an adult with ADHD, some of your emotional scar tissue may come from years of being told you're not enough in some way. You may wonder whether you have ADHD or if those voices are just right about you.

I hope that by this point, you see that you're not alone. I hope that you see there is a path forward to organize your chaos, take control of the spotlight in the circus, and enjoy your day at the proverbial beach without being carried away in the tide.

Most of all, I hope that you have begun to believe that your path forward is your own, no matter what your diagnosis says or whether anyone else believes you.

There's an interesting phenomenon in the body called the placebo effect.

Etymologically, *placebo* is in the future tense, meaning "I *will* please." In medicine, placebos are often used in controlled trials. Half the trial group is given a new medication and half is given a placebo, often in the form of a pill, that contains no medication.

The two groups are then compared over time to see if the medication actually does what it was intended to do.

However, a surprisingly high number of cases, maybe one in three, experience this "placebo effect." People feel better or are cured, even if they are in the control group and the "medication" they are taking has no active ingredient.

This means many people taking placebo antidepressants become significantly less depressed, even if there is no pharmacological reason. In the United Kingdom, in fact, antidepressants are no longer immediately prescribed in government-run hospitals for the treatment of mild to moderate depression—exercise, meditation, and CBT are the treatments of choice, knowing that the pill itself isn't always changing the body in the way that these treatments do.

But the placebo effect goes further and deeper than that. One study was done on knee surgeries performed for patients with osteoarthritis. Some of the patients received the standard knee operation. Others simply had their knees opened and sewn back with no actual surgery performed.

The people who received the placebo treatment walked and climbed better during the first year than those who actually had the surgery. Two years after the surgery, there was no difference in results between those who had the real surgery and those who had the placebo surgery.[45]

This tells us something remarkable about the mind's influence on the body and our emotional state.

Yet many people misunderstand the word *placebo*, associating it with "fake," when what's happening is very real.

The point here is that what others understand to be true about you and your symptoms and your treatment plan are not as important about what you know to be true about yourself.

Remember, you're in a lifelong relationship with ADHD—there is no "cure."

I've emphasized many ways of dealing with the challenges of ADHD in this book because it's necessary to create a toolbox full of options for the mind that will influence your body and emotional state for the better.

You could call medication, therapy, exercise, and mindfulness placebos if you'd like. But you can also call them effective tools for rising up to the executive-function challenges associated with ADHD. All the tools explored in this book can have a significant impact on your life and mental, emotional, and physiological states and are worth exploring as you create your personal path forward.

The LMNOP philosophy advises you to find your own personalized, inner placebo. What is it that empowers you to make shifts at times when you're feeling stuck? For many people, this means heading to the gym. For others, it involves mindfulness meditation. I may download an app on my phone that's meant to help me with time management. But those tools will only be effective if I use them in ways that work for me.

We have to find the things in our lives, whatever their intrinsic merit, that work for us personally. And they'll only work if you invest yourself in them—if you invest your time and energy and incredible capacity for creativity *on you.*

For these tools to work, you need to believe in them and believe in yourself.

I know I do. It's time to refocus your ADHD until you believe in you too.

Conclusion

Two trends are on the rise. One is the increased diagnosis of ADHD in both children and adults. The second is the proliferation of technology and research showing its deleterious effects on our attention, focus, and productivity—what I've called Techno-ADD. This has created an increasing need for perspective, self-reflection, and the tools to effectively manage both clinical ADHD and Techno-ADD.

This book has focused on complementary, supplementary, and alternative tools for managing the condition's challenges, though medication remains a viable and valuable tool as well.

Behavioral-modification techniques include using a 3-Tier planning system for more effective time management, and communication techniques designed to improve clarity and reduce misunderstanding. Cognitive therapy focuses on an increasing awareness of maladaptive thinking patterns and strategies to help you restructure them.

Mindfulness is really this approach's overarching philosophy, and the related techniques for self-compassion and yogic breathing have genuinely helped me and many of my ADHD clients.

Both those with clinical ADHD and Techno-ADD will also benefit from creating breaks and buffers in their use of technology—working especially on improving your relationship with your phone. Set up boundaries, designate tech-free zones, and avoid sleeping with the phone in the bedroom. You might even be so bold as to turn your phone off for an entire day a week, or at least for an evening.

For all of these symptom-management and brain-training techniques, don't forget to take stock of some of the positive sides and advantages of ADHD. These include the capacity to hyperfocus and get into a creative flow, and the fact that adults with ADHD often experience high levels of energy and passion.

It cannot be said enough: ADHD is a lifelong condition. It's also unlikely we're going to eliminate our use of attention-deteriorating technology. We must therefore learn to live in balance with both, and the steps presented in this book can help you move forward on that path toward a more organized, refocused future.

But how to follow those steps? Conduct an experiment. Commit yourself to experimenting with three of these techniques for one to three months and see what happens.

Which three techniques? That's ultimately up to you. However, if forced to narrow it down, my favorite steps—the ones that have worked best for both me and my clients—would be the 3-Tier time-management system (Chapter 10), mindfulness meditation (Chapter 18), and cognitive restructuring (Chapter 14).

Use the full 3-Tier System—weekly, daily, and hourly—for at least a month. Once you see its many benefits and the changes it makes in your life, you'll almost certainly want to keep using it. Don't forget to incorporate fifteen- to thirty-minute buffers when planning your schedule!

Then explore mindfulness meditation. It's probably easiest to begin by choosing an app such as Headspace, Ten Percent Happier, Calm, Insight Timer, or Waking Up. Try both guided and unguided meditation and see what works best for you. Begin with three to five minutes of daily meditation and build up from there.

If you can build up to ten minutes a day, you're a rock star. By the same token, be forgiving of yourself. If you can't meditate daily, meditate as many days in a week as you can. Daily practice may be the ultimate goal, but engagement is the realistic goal. Just engage with mindfulness.

Finally, it never hurts to be reminded that just because you think something doesn't mean it's true. As part of your experiment, try a cognitive restructuring tool, either an app like Woebot or a workbook like *Mind Over Mood*.

Always remember that 80 is the new 100. To think you need to hit 100 percent is to put yourself under pressure fraught with pitfalls and self-recrimination. Aiming for a 60 to 80 percent success rate on your intentions in a day is a noble enough goal and worth celebrating when you reach it. If you simultaneously widen the bull's-eye *and* maintain better focus, you'll find greater contentment while living your fullest life.

Once you've experimented with these ABCs of mindful ADHD reorganization, develop the LMNOPs: live mindfully, notice opportunity, and personalize your path. It's good advice for anyone, but especially for those of us who are living with, meeting, and overcoming the challenges of adult ADHD.

Acknowledgments

This book was a winding labor of love (and procrastination ;-)). It was made that much easier with the support of many along the way.

To my parents, Frieda and Eddie^{A"H}, this book is a testament to your willingness to unconditionally be my greatest cheerleaders. Mom, as the first adult with ADHD I ever knew, I thank you for highlighting ADHD's positive aspects through your emotional intelligence, uninhibited personality, and encouragement to color outside the lines. My father passed away in 2020, midway through my work on this book. He was best known for his integrity, structure, and focus. His lists, reminders, and pocket calendar are the model of organization that I strive toward. Thank you, Pop.

To my wife Ayla, thank you for your unwavering support and encouragement to never give up despite stumbles, tumbles, and turns. You are a rock of consistency and love.

Thank you to my friends and family for checking in with me as

I immersed myself in this project, always reminding me not to stop until I hit the finish line. Thank you to my colleagues and students at Baruch College for fostering a warm environment of intellectual striving and academic excellence that served as the backdrop for my efforts with this book.

This book could not have come into being without the help of my team at Scribe. In particular, Tom Lane, who helped get this book out of my brain and onto paper. Libby Allen, for keeping a watchful eye and helping all elements fall into place for this book to be published. And most notably, to my incomparable scribe and editor-of-all, Brannan Sirratt. You put your everything into this book with brilliance, care, and compassion. Sure, you picked up the ADHD diagnosis along the way too, and opted to fold it right back into the project through personal insights and excitement to help others flourish.

I am grateful to my mentors, Dr. Susan Locke, Rabbi Joseph Dweck, Dr. David Pelcovitz, Hari Kaur, and Joseph Beyda[A"H]. Your collective wisdom, inspiration, and guidance over the years continue to light my path forward.

Finally, I want to give a special mention to my dear friend DJ Cohen[A"H]. DJ was diagnosed with pancreatic cancer in 2015, and despite being given a three-month prognosis, he manifested four inspirational years of life, love, and light, impacting this world in exponential ways. Throughout those years, DJ constantly pushed me to start this book project, and it was the promise I made to him to do so that ultimately sparked me into action. Deej—many thanks for always being thankful, present, and aware.

About the Author

DAVID SITT, PsyD, is a man of many hats, with a passion for lighting the path toward optimal living. As a tenured professor at Baruch College (CUNY), he exposes undergraduate students to psychology, cutting-edge research, and the mysteries of the brain. At the graduate level, he trains the next generation of therapists in CBT. As a clinician, he specializes in treating adults with ADHD, anxiety, and mood disorders through validated modalities and innovative techniques. As a consultant and executive coach, Dr. Sitt advises thought leaders, corporations, and educational institutions and has been featured on Vice Media, the *Howard Stern Show*, and in the *New York Times*. He and his wife live in Brooklyn with their four children. To learn more, visit drsitt.com.

Notes

CHAPTER 1

1   *DSM* stands for the *Diagnostic and Statistical Manual of Mental Disorders*, which the American Psychiatric Association compiles to assist in the diagnosis of ADHD and other psychological and psychiatric conditions. This was from the fourth edition of the book, which is now in its fifth edition and updated in 2022 to *DSM-V-TR*.

2   Faraone, S. V., Asherson, P., Banaschewski, T., Biederman, J., Buitelaar, J. K., Ramos-Quiroga, J. A., Rohde, L. A., Sonuga-Barke, E. J. S., Tannock, R., & Franke, B. (2015). Attention-deficit/hyperactivity disorder. *Nature Reviews Disease Primers 1*(15020). https://doi.org/10.1038/nrdp.2015.20; Owens, E. B., Cardoos, S. L., & Hinshaw, S. P. (2015). Developmental progression and gender differences among individuals with ADHD. In Barkley, R. A. (Ed.), *Attention deficit hyperactivity disorder: A handbook for diagnosis and treatment* (4th ed., pp. 223–255). Guilford Press.

CHAPTER 2

3   Uchida, M., Spencer, T. J., Faraone, S. V., & Biederman, J. (2018). Adult outcome of ADHD: An overview of results from the MGH longitudinal family studies of pediatrically and psychiatrically referred youth with and without ADHD of both sexes. *Journal of Attention Disorders, 22*(6), 523–534. https://doi.org/10.1177/1087054715604360

CHAPTER 3

4   Faraone, S. V., & Larsson, H. (2019). Genetics of attention deficit hyperactivity disorder. *Molecular Phsychiatry, 24*(4), 562–575. https://doi.org/10.1038/s41380-018-0070-0

5   Barkley, R. A. (2017). *What causes ADHD?* RusselBarkley.org. http://www.russellbarkley.org/factsheets/WhatCausesADHD2017.pdf

6   Cortese, S. (2012). The neurobiology and genetics of attention-deficit/hyperactivity disorder (ADHD): What every clinician should know. *European Journal of Paediatric Neurology, 16*(5), 422–433. https://doi.org/10.1016/j.ejpn.2012.01.009

7   Barkley, R. A. (2017). *What causes ADHD?* RusselBarkley.org. http://www.russellbarkley.org/factsheets/WhatCausesADHD2017.pdf

8   Uchida, M., Driscoll, H., DiSalvo, M., Rajalakshmim, A., Maiello, M., Spera, V., & Biederman, J. (2021). Assessing the magnitude of risk for ADHD in offspring of parents with ADHD: A systematic literature review and meta-analysis. *Journal of Attention Disorders, 25*(13), 1943–1948. https://doi.org/10.1177/1087054720950815

9   Sagvolden, T., Johansen, E. B., Aase, H., & Russell, V. A. (2005). A dynamic developmental theory of attention-deficit/hyperactivity disorder (ADHD) predominantly hyperactive/impulsive and combined subtypes. *Behavioral and Brain Sciences, 28*(3), 397–419. https://doi.org/10.1017/S0140525X05000075

10 Banerjee, E., & Nandagopal, K. (2015). Does serotonin deficit mediate susceptibility to ADHD? *Neurochemistry International, 82*, 52–68. https://doi.org/10.1016/j.neuint.2015.02.001

11 Barkley, R. A. (2017). *When an adult you love has ADHD: Professional advice for parents, partners, and siblings.* American Psychological Association. https://doi.org/10.1037/15963-000

12 Rubia, K., Smith, A. B., Brammer, M. J., Toone, B., & Taylor, E. (2005). Abnormal brain activation during inhibition and error detection in medication-naive adolescents with ADHD. *The American Journal of Psychiatry, 162*(6), 1067–1075. https://doi.org/10.1176/appi.ajp.162.6.1067; Castellanos, F. X., Lee, P. P., Sharp, W., Jeffries, N. O., Greenstein, D. K., Clasen, L. S., Blumenthal, J. D., James, R. S., Ebens, C. L., Walter, J. M., Zijdenbos, A., Evans, A. C., Giedd, J. N., & Rapoport, J. L. (2002). Developmental trajectories of brain volume abnormalities in children and adolescents with attention-deficit/hyperactivity disorder. *JAMA, 288*(14), 1740–1748. https://doi.org/10.1001/jama.288.14.1740; Shaw, P., Greenstein, D., Lerch, J., Clasen, L., Lenroot, R., Gogtay, N., Evans, A., Rapoport, J., & Giedd, J. (2006). Intellectual ability and cortical development in children and adolescents. *Nature, 440*(7084), 676–679. https://doi.org/10.1038/nature04513

13 Spencer, T. J., Biederman, J., & Mick, E. (2007). Attention-deficit/hyperactivity disorder: Diagnosis, lifespan, comorbidities, and neurobiology. *Journal of Pediatric Psychology, 32*(6), 631–642. https://doi.org/10.1093/jpepsy/jsm005

14 George, M. J., Russell, M. A., Piontak, J. R., & Odgers, C. L. (2018). Concurrent and subsequent associations between daily digital technology use and high-risk adolescents' mental health symptoms. *Child Development, 89*(1), 78–88. https://doi.org/10.1111/cdev.12819

15 Ra, C. K., Cho, J., Stone, M. D., De La Cerda, J., Goldenson, N. I., Moroney, E., Tung, I., Lee, S. S., & Leventhal, A. M. (2018). Association of digital media use with subsequent symptoms of attention-deficit/hyperactivity disorder among adolescents. *JAMA, 320*(3), 255–263. https://doi.org/10.1001/jama.2018.8931

CHAPTER 4

16 Barkley, R. A., & Fischer, M. (2019). Hyperactive child syndrome and estimated life expectancy at young adult follow-up: The role of ADHD persistence and other potential predictors. *Journal of Attention Disorders, 23*(9), 907–923. https://doi.org/10.1177/1087054718816164

17 Ra, C. K., Cho, J., Stone, M. D., De La Cerda, J., Goldenson, N. I., Moroney, E., Tung, I., Lee, S. S., & Leventhal, A. M. (2018). Association of digital media use with subsequent symptoms of attention-deficit/hyperactivity disorder among adolescents. *JAMA, 320*(3), 255–263. https://doi.org/10.1001/jama.2018.8931

CHAPTER 5

18 Caye, A., Rocha, T. B., Anselmi, L., Murray, J., Menezes, A. M. B., Barros, F. C., Gonçalves, H., Wehrmeister, F., Jensen, C. M., Steinhausen, H., Swanson, J. M., Kieling, C., & Rohde, L. A. (2016). Attention-deficit/hyperactivity disorder trajectories from childhood to young adulthood: Evidence from a birth cohort supporting a late-onset syndrome. *JAMA Psychiatry, 73*(7), 705–712. https://doi.org/10.1001/jamapsychiatry.2016.0383; Faraone, S. V., & Biederman, J. (2016). Can attention-deficit/hyperactivity disorder onset occur in adulthood? *JAMA Psychiatry, 73*(7), 655–656. https://doi.org/10.1001/jamapsychiatry.2016.0400

CHAPTER 8

19 While we are going to refer to this novel idea as "Techno-ADD" because it flows well, we are NOT excluding the propensity for impulsive/hyperactive symptoms to be included, as explained in the pages to come.

20 *Black Mirror* explores the potential of technology, for better or worse, in many ways. But season 1, episode 3, "The Entire History of You" (2011) is particularly relevant to this conversation.

21 Nielsen. (2018, July). *Time flies: U.S. adults now spend nearly half a day interacting with media.* https://www.nielsen.com/insights/2018/time-flies-us-adults-now-spend-nearly-half-a-day-interacting-with-media/

22 Kepios. (n.d.). *Global social media statistics.* DataReportal. https://datareportal.com/social-media-users

23 Longstreet, P., & Brooks, S. (2017). Life satisfaction: A key to managing internet and social media addiction. *Technology in Society, 50,* 73–77. https://doi.org/10.1016/j.techsoc.2017.05.003

24 FameMass. (n.d.). *Latest social media addiction statistics of 2023 [new data].* https://famemass.com/social-media-addiction-statistics/

25 Glass, A., & Kang, M. (2019). Dividing attention in the classroom reduces exam performance. *Educational Psychology, 39*(3), 395–408. https://doi.org/10.1080/01443410.2018.1489046

26 Yellman, M. A., Bryan, L., Sauber-Schatz, E. K., & Brener, N. (2020). Transportation risk behaviors among high school students: Youth risk behavior survey, United States, 2019. *MMWR Supplements, 69*(1), 77–83. http://dx.doi.org/10.15585/mmwr.su6901a9

27 "The term digital immigrant mostly applies to individuals who were born before the spread of the digital technology and who were not exposed to it at an early age. Digital natives are the opposite of digital immigrants, they have been interacting with technology from childhood." Henderson, C. (2020, August 21). *What does it mean to be a digital native.* Medium. https://medium.com/@@colinhenderson/what-does-it-mean-to-be-a-digital-native-cd66e9407cba

CHAPTER 9

28 Wheelwright, T. (2022, January 24). *2022 Cell phone usage statistics: How obsessed are we?* Reviews.org. https://www.reviews.org/mobile/cell-phone-addiction/

29 Turkle, S. (2011). *Alone together: Why we expect more from technology and less from each other.* Basic Books.

CHAPTER 10

30 Mueller, P. A., & Oppenheimer, D. M. (2016). Technology and note-taking in the classroom, boardroom, hospital room, and courtroom. *Trends in Neuroscience and Education, 5*(3), 139–145. https://doi.org/10.1016/j.tine.2016.06.002

CHAPTER 14

31   Knouse, L. E., Zvorsky, I., & Safren, S. A. (2013). Depression in adults with attention-deficit/hyperactivity disorder (ADHD): The mediating role of cognitive-behavioral factors. *Cognitive Therapy and Research, 37*(6), 1220–1232. https://doi.org/10.1007/s10608-013-9569-5

CHAPTER 15

32   Greenberger, D., & Padesky, C. (2016). *Mind over mood: Change how you feel by changing the way you think* (2nd ed.). Guildford Press.

CHAPTER 16

33   Kabat-Zinn, J. (1982). An outpatient program in behavioral medicine for chronic pain patients based on the practice of mindfulness meditation: Theoretical considerations and preliminary results. *General Hospital Psychiatry, 4*(1), 33–47. https://doi.org/10.1016/0163-8343(82)90026-3

34   Segal, Z. V., Williams, J. M. G., & Teasdale, J. D. (2002). *Mindfulness-based cognitive therapy for depression: A new approach to preventing relapse.* Guilford Press.

35   Aadil, M., Cosme, R. M., & Chernaik, J. (2017). Mindfulness-based cognitive behavioral therapy as an adjunct treatment of attention deficit hyperactivity disorder in young adults: A literature review. *Cureus, 9*(5), e1269. https://doi.org/10.7759/cureus.1269; Bachmann, K., Lam, A. P., & Philipsen, A. (2016). Mindfulness-based cognitive therapy and the adult ADHD brain: A neuropsychotherapeutic perspective. *Frontiers in Psychiatry, 7,* 117. https://doi.org/10.3389/fpsyt.2016.00117; Zylowska, L., Ackerman, D. L., Yang, M. H., Futrell, J. L., Horton, N. L., Hale, T. S., Pataki, C., & Smalley, S. L. (2008). Mindfulness meditation training in adults and adolescents with ADHD: A feasibility study. *Journal of Attention Disorders, 11*(6), 737–746. https://doi.org/10.1177/1087054707308502

36   This is from an October 2022 report entitled *The U.S. meditation market* issued by Marketdata LLC, a leading independent market research publisher since 1979. The study traces the market from 2015 to 2019, with projections for 2022 and 2025, examining these services and products: Meditation Centers/Studios, Retreats, Books, Smartphone Apps, Websites, Online Courses, Employer Programs, DVDs, and CDs. https://www.marketresearch.com/Marketdata-Enterprises-Inc-v416/Meditation-32339827/?progid=91794

37   LaRosa, J. (2017, September 26). *$1.2 billion U.S. meditation market to grow strongly, following path of yoga studios.* WebWire. https://www.webwire.com/ViewPressRel.asp?aId=214152

38   Zylowska, L. (2012). *The mindfulness prescription for adult ADHD: An eight-step program for strengthening attention, managing emotions, and achieving your goals.* Trumpeter.

CHAPTER 19

39 Barkley, R. A. (2017). *When an adult you love has ADHD: Professional advice for parents, partners, and siblings.* American Psychological Association. https://doi.org/10.1037/15963-000

40 Chiu, H. J., Sun, C. K., Fan, H. Y., Tzang, R. F., Wang, M. Y., Cheng, Y. C., Cheng, Y. S., Yeh, P. Y., & Chung, W. (2022). Surface electroencephalographic neurofeedback improves sustained attention in ADHD: A meta-analysis of randomized controlled trials. *Child and Adolescent Psychiatry and Mental Health, 16*(1), 104. https://doi.org/10.1186/s13034-022-00543-1

CHAPTER 20

41 Cerrillo-Urbina, A. J., García-Hermoso, A., Sánchez-López, M., Pardo-Guijarro, M. J., Santos Gómez, J. L., & Martínez-Vizcaíno, V. (2015). The effects of physical exercise in children with attention deficit hyperactivity disorder: A systematic review and meta-analysis of randomized control trials. *Child : Care, Health & Development, 41*(6), 779–788. https://doi.org/10.1111/cch.12255

42 Mehren, A., Özyurt, J., Lam, A. P., Brandes, M., Müller, H. H. O., Thiel, C. M., & Philipsen, A. (2019). Acute effects of aerobic exercise on executive function and attention in adult patients with ADHD. *Frontiers in Psychiatry, 10*, 132. https://doi.org/10.3389/fpsyt.2019.00132; Klil-Drori, S., & Hechtman, L. (2020). Potential social and neurocognitive benefits of aerobic exercise as adjunct treatment for patients with ADHD. *Journal of Attention Disorders, 24*(5), 795–809. https://doi.org/10.1177/1087054716652617

43 Den Heijer, A. E., Groen, Y., Tucha, L., Fuermaier, A. B., Koerts, J., Lange, K. W., Thome, J., & Tucha, O. (2017). Sweat it out? The effects of physical exercise on cognition and behavior in children and adults with ADHD: A systematic literature review. *Journal of Neural Transmission, 124*(Supplement 1), 3–26. https://doi.org/10.1007/s00702-016-1593-7

44 Berwid, O. G., & Halperin, J. M. (2012). Emerging support for a role of exercise in attention-deficit/hyperactivity disorder intervention planning. *Current Psychiatry Reports, 14*(5), 543–551. https://doi.org/10.1007/s11920-012-0297-4

CHAPTER 22

45 Sihvonen, R., Paavola, M., Malmivaara, A., Itälä, A., Joukainen, A., Nurmi, H., Kalske, J., & Järvinen, T. L. N. (2013). Arthroscopic partial meniscectomy versus sham surgery for a degenerative meniscal tear. *New England Journal of Medicine, 369*(26), 2515–2524. https://doi.org/10.1056/nejmoa1305189

Printed in the USA
CPSIA information can be obtained
at www.ICGtesting.com
LVHW090914090324
774032LV00007B/133